PRAYING THE PATHWAY TO PEACE

PRAYER BEGINS WITH SILENCE

SILENCE LEADS TO THE LOVE OF GOD

THE LOVE OF GOD LEADS TO THE LOVE OF NEIGHBOR

THE LOVE OF NEIGHBOR LEADS TO REPENTANCE

REPENTANCE LEADS TO GRACE

GRACE LEADS TO GENEROSITY

GENEROSITY LEADS TO PEACE

Billy Still is the author of *The Jawbone of a Carnivore – Praying the Pathway to Peace*, a book for people with spiritual questions and an interest in adventure. Billy has spent his life as a pastor, husband, father, adventurer, wilderness traveler, ultra-athlete, and one who struggles to identify prayer in the ways we move through life. He is recently retired and in his retirement has earned the Solstice MFA in Creative Nonfiction from Pine Manor College. Billy and his wife, Ann, have spent their life together in Mississippi, Alaska, and Arizona, where they currently live.

To Ann, my extraordinary wife, companion, and friend, who never fails to embrace the beauty of our adventures and who is always eager for life's next chapter. To Anne-Marie Oomen, my writing mentor and friend, who more than once said, "This is good. If good is enough for you, stop now; or if you like, we can move on to excellence." After which I headed to my study for one more revision. I dedicate this book to both of you and offer my deepest gratitude.

Billy Still

THE JAWBONE OF A CARNIVORE

Praying the Pathway to Peace

AUSTIN MACAULEY PUBLISHERS™

LONDON • CAMBRIDGE • NEW YORK • SHARJAH

A CIP catalogue record for this title is available from the British Library.

ISBN 9781528914420 (Paperback)
ISBN 9781528960892 (ePub e-book)

www.austinmacauley.com

First Published (2019)
Austin Macauley Publishers Ltd
25 Canada Square
Canary Wharf
London
E14 5LQ

The Jawbone of a Carnivore is the story of a particular flow of events that reflect the continuing formation of my praying self. It is not the story of my life. The tales told here are not in chronological order, neither are they an attempt to document the most significant people I have known or the moments we shared. Therefore many, if not most, of the people who helped form my life and character are not mentioned in its pages. The book to tell all of you thanks would be far too long. Let me offer these words of gratitude. I am overwhelmingly grateful to all those who have called me family, pastor, and friend. Whatever I have accomplished in my life is the result of your confident and unconditional love. I am also grateful to the community of writers associated with the Solstice MFA, Pine Manor College. We fell in love, not only with each other's writing, but with each other's deep desire to find ourselves alive on the page. Thank you all.

Table of Contents

A Letter to My Readers

My breath forms a solid cloud in front of my face. A sub-arctic February night. Two a.m., I stumble down an embankment and onto the frozen surface of Alaska's Yentna River, miles from a road. Our varying paces have separated me from my friends and I am alone, yet not really alone. At this moment, I feel fully alive. I take a step forward, and the frost crushing under my feet sounds like thin glass shattering on brick. This is the Iditasport 100 Mile Endurance Run. I am propelled forward into the frozen dark night. Confident, content, and permeated with a sense of wonder, to be here, this cold, this alive: this is a prayer.

Prayer has been a stranger to me most of my life. This seems odd, even to me. I am a Christian and a pastor. I pray in public and in private. I teach people how to pray and lead groups in prayer exercises. I have read countless books about prayer, have queried folks whom I know to be heartfelt prayers and have taught myself to sit in silence while meditating on a few short words. Still, none of this comes naturally to me. At the same time, I have a vigorous relationship with God and our active closeness guides my life. In my quest to understand the contradiction between my struggle with prayer and my closeness to God, I have recognized two things about myself: 1. I talk too quickly and too much. Many times I have talked over significant events or failed to hear what others have to say. On more than one occasion, I have sent someone away wounded because I spoke too quickly and with a self-assurance unearned by careful consideration. 2. I am at peace when I move, and when I move,

11

I am finally silent. As an ultrarunner, cyclist, adventurer, and explorer, I spend a great deal of time alone, and even when I have companions, we are frequently too engaged in what we are doing to talk about it. These are the moments when I experience the most recognizable vitality in my relationship with God and others. What I have concluded is that for me, movement represents my best way of praying. In my quest to come to a deeper understanding of this moving-praying phenomenon in my life, I began to explore my spiritual life in a different way.

One fall when I was the pastor of St. Paul's United Methodist Church in Tucson, Arizona, I invited our church program staff to accompany me on a retreat where we would explore these matters. The purpose of the retreat was for each of us to identify the roadblocks to peace in our lives and then to identify our personal pathway to peace. Perhaps if we could identify the patterns that were consistent in our lives, they would provide a roadmap we could trust on a difficult day. I could imagine myself saying: "Oh yeah. When this happens to me, for it to have the greatest meaning, I must recognize where it leads." I suspected that each movement of the spiritual life leads somewhere, and nothing is an end within itself. I came to learn that there are predictable patterns in my spiritual life that dictate how I pray, how I experience adventure, as well as my relationship with God and others.

Within my community of trusted friends, we eagerly shared our findings with each other. I will share mine with you, the particular pattern that works for me, and I invite you to join me as it becomes the heart of this book, The Jawbone of a Carnivore, Praying the Pathway to Peace.

Prayer begins with silence

Silence leads to the love of God

The love of God leads to the love of neighbor

The love of neighbor leads to repentance

Repentance leads to grace

Grace leads to generosity

Generosity leads to peace

Each of these understandings has become markers on my pathway to peace. Identifying them provides me with a sense of assurance, confidence, and direction, even when the markers on the pathway to peace are recognized in retrospect.

This is not a book of instructions on how to pray, rather a recognition that the way we live our lives can become a prayer. This memoir is ordered around the pathway to peace that provides way markers for my moving, praying life. You will find tales of adventure, friendship, eccentric people, success, and failure, as well as encounters with life and death. This particular pathway to peace raises more questions than it answers. It trusts that you will strike out on your own adventuresome exploration of the spiritual life. Perhaps, through this, you will identify your pathway to peace and in so doing find yourself saying on some cold and snowy morning, "This is a prayer."

Grace and peace, Billy Still

The Descent of Mount Logan

Before the sound of my buddies' cars, crunching on the ice-covered street, quite faded in the distance, I discovered my lovely Ann, sullen and tearful, sitting at the kitchen table, a tissue to her cheek. I'd walked my eager friends to their cars: we were ebullient, alive, and buoyed with optimism, captured by our wild dreams. Ann had heard it all.

My adventuring friends had been visiting our home in Anchorage, Alaska. While Ann had a certain affection for each of these men, she recognized that they were dangerous people, full of tempestuous notions and undaunted by the idea that some feats of adventure lay beyond our grasp. As Will, Bob, Dave, and I sat around visualizing daring exploits in the Alaskan wilderness, Ann listened and thought about the impact on home, job, three children, and herself. This had been the kind of night that inevitably left my imagination soaring. It was the kind of night that did just the opposite for my loving, responsible, literal-minded, accountant wife.

I stopped just inside the doorway, gauging the shift in mood, "Hey, babe, what's wrong?"

"What's wrong? What do you think is wrong?" She didn't wait for an answer. She knew that I had no idea why she was upset. "Did you hear yourself tonight? You guys are going to kayak Prince William Sound, run the Alaska Wilderness Classic, ski the Harding Icefield, raft the Koyukuk River, and climb Mount Logan! How in the world will we pay for this?

You'll be gone all the time, perhaps lose your job, and what if something happens to you?"

I was stunned. It had never occurred to me, or any of these guys, that we would do all of this, at least not in the same year.

"Awww, Ann," I said in a conciliatory tone she must have distrusted by that time in our marriage. "I'm sorry. We are not going to do all of that. We were just trying them out to see which idea will survive as our next big adventure?"

"That's not what you said."

"No, it's not," I conceded. Ann has this gift for remembering conversations with startling exactitude.

"You want to do all of that." It was a fact.

"Yes, I do, but not right away." Trying to defuse the situation and temper her distress, I downplayed our eager excitement to be outside, on a wild trail. Somewhere. Out there.

But it was an ongoing concern for both of us.

Within a few days, Ann and I regained clarity about our different ways of understanding the world. She blessed my need for adventure and I her strong sense of order. Our deep affection for each other provided the assurance that peace would be restored. That said, by the next summer, after countless three-day adventures, and endless arguments with friends on the trail, Mount Logan won the competition for our adventuring affection. The largest, most remote mountain in North America was to be mine. As always, Ann gave her cautious blessing.

I went to Mount Logan looking for adventure, but I was also always searching for that peace and redemption I found in intense movement, and perhaps to forge a future in the high mountains. I have been a pastor all of my adult life. I have also been a church builder, a husband and parent, a firefighter/rescue climber, an ultrarunner, cyclist, athlete, adventurer, and a person who has lived with heart disease since my late thirties. Despite the contradictions embedded in that list, I was in search of patterns and order in the context of life's defining stories, markers clarifying the trajectory of my journey on the pathway to peace.

I thrive on adventure and join those who throughout history have noted the positive correlation between our struggles as adventurers and the quest for peace in our personal lives. As a young adult, I read the history of Mallory and Irvine, Eric Shipton and Bill Tilman, their courageous attempts to summit Mount Everest as well as their wanderers' pact with the other European explorers of the Himalayas. I know the details of the failed Franklin Expedition and their quest for the Northwest Passage, and I think of Roald Amundsen as the last Viking. It seems to me that Ernest Shackleton and Sir Douglas Mawson wrote of their pursuit of the South Pole as if it were the Holy Grail. Their willingness to embrace suffering took them to the absolute limits of human possibility. Their accomplishments remain an overwhelming inspiration to me. These folks affirmed the longing many of us carry in our hearts to move beyond a simple reflection on beauty, to embrace the struggle inherent in traveling through remote, isolated environments. As we find our way in some of the world's wildest places, the relationship between struggle and peace becomes strikingly clear.

Folks who are afraid of wild places often see them as alien locales through which they must reluctantly pass. It is true that if you view them as your enemy, you are likely to be defeated. A mountain, glacier, river, even a bear has no sense of kindness or mercy to offer you. They exist within highly defined parameters of life. When you choose to understand them, accept them, and move, without resistance, within boundaries of cooperation, you become part of the environment. When you struggle against them, you find them to be a source of anxiety, fear, and ultimately, defeat. It is a lesson I continue to learn over time, recognizing its nuances in each adventure.

Mount Logan is one of those wild places. We had no desire to challenge her. We longed to embrace her. Found in the St. Elias Mountain Range in Canada's Yukon Territory, at 5,959 meters/19,550 feet, it is second in height in North America only to Alaska's Denali. Far more remote than Denali, when measured by its circumference, it is considered the largest non-volcanic mountain on earth. Approximately 1200 mountaineers a year attempt to climb Denali, while no more than 75 to 100 climbers a year attempt Mount Logan. Part of the difficulty of Mount Logan is its remoteness. The other difficulty is its eccentric summit plateau, which is 20 kilometers long and 5 kilometers wide. It is completely exposed and constantly battered by horrific winds. At times, it is the coldest place on earth outside of Antarctica. Mount Logan is white, and it is terrifying. Until you reach the summit plateau, no sign of a rock or anything else mars the ice and snow. Its blank beauty seems to go on forever.

An epic decision greets the climber who considers Mount Logan's summit plateau. One of two choices must be made on summit day. You can make a single day, alpine push for the summit. This means you carry a light pack, cross the summit plateau, climb the summit, and return. You cannot stop on this journey. It is far too cold to stand around, and your light pack does not have room for the equipment required for an overnight bivouac. Your other choice is to take a full pack, still light but up to forty pounds, and get close to the base of the summit. Then you climb down over the edge of the plateau ridge and make camp. Since you have worked to keep your pack light, you do not have a tent so you must dig a shelter. At the lower elevations of the mountain, you can take your plastic avalanche shovel and dig in the snow. Here the wind is so constant that there is little snow, only ice. Ice axe in hand, you chip away. This is whip-hard work, and in the frigid cold you work fast. You don't dig much of a cave, just enough to provide a platform for your stove, sleeping bag, and shelter from the wind. You struggle between conserving energy and doing things right. The next day, you climb the summit and return to your camp. On the third day, you return to the descent of the ridge. Both of these pathways are difficult and filled with risk. A number of climbers have died on Mount Logan, almost all of them on the descent when exhaustion overwhelms common sense and thinking turns to mud. Like everyone who goes to Mount Logan, we spent a considerable amount of time around kitchen tables spread with maps, or on trails, our gestures always debating these summiting options.

I would be with my friends Bob, Will, and Dave. We were also joined by George, a man I did not know. All of us were experienced mountaineers and wilderness travelers. Snow, cold, mountain storms, and glaciers did not intimidate us, and we were eager to embrace the suffering promised by a trip to Mount Logan.

My friends had another significant reason for this trip. They believed that they were there to contribute to my healing. It was 1994. In 1991, I had spent the year in a surprising struggle with coronary artery disease. At thirty-seven, I had three heart catheterizations in a period of six months. In the early 1990s, things like angioplasty and atherectomy were revolutionary. No one had a clear idea of how effective they would be over time. Today these procedures seem commonplace. On occasion, they are even performed as outpatient procedures. In those days, an angioplasty required several days in the hospital and at least one night in ICU.

At that time, the idea of placing a stent inside a coronary artery was still far in the future. My surgeon told me that I should expect to require another intervention somewhere between eighteen months and ten years. Thus, the adventure cure, here and now. Timid and fearful souls encouraged me to find new and safer outlets for my energy, but these guys were not among them. As I gradually returned to my previous level of adventure seeking, these friends were confident that this type of quest provided the pathway to new life. I agreed with them. All of the things that made Mount Logan uniquely difficult in the world of mountaineering were the reasons we were there.

Even Ann had agreed.

We flew onto Mount Logan's massive ice field in June, aboard a de Havilland Canada DHC-2 Beaver, a single-engine, high-wing, propeller-driven airplane that has the largest carrying capacity of any bush plane. We delivered all our equipment in one flight. Our pilot was Paul Klaus, a well-known bush pilot whose family owns and works out of Ultima Thule Lodge. His experience guaranteed he knew the dangers we faced—guaranteed he knew that we must have had more heart than good sense. We did not mention my compromised heart to him. Too many people discouraged me once they heard that part of my story. It was my decision. I had chosen the risk. Only those of us on the adventure would know.

On any beautiful and clear day, you cannot see the summit of Mount Logan from the glaciers below, but you can see the line of the summit plateau rise above you. It is an overwhelming scene of fierce intimidation. No matter how lovely the day, the weather is always unstable. A blue sky can swirl into storm in minutes. Because of that potential, we immediately made camp. We had a limited number of tents, and we did not want to set them up and take them down each day. Since we would be creating camps up and down the mountain, we chose to use snow caves instead of tents in our base camp. A lot of snow had fallen the week before, and it had consolidated, making it firm and stable. And easy to dig. Everyone had a plastic avalanche shovel, important tools for making camp, and even more critical if someone should be buried in an avalanche. If everyone has a shovel, a chance exists to dig them out.

Today we were simply digging into the side of a ridge of snow. You dig in about three feet and then begin to dig at a right angle. This means the entrance will protect you from the fierce Logan winds. Starting in the side of the ridge gives you confidence that your cave will be stable. You know that while a storm can block the entrance to a snow cave, if dug properly it will never collapse, and it is easy to dig out. We dug several caves for sleeping and another to store extra food and gear. As we dug a cooking area, we began with a large pit about six feet across and seven feet deep. This provided room to stand in to cook and eat, and we would be protected from the wind. This also made it easier to use our stove, since there would be no wind blowing the flame from side to side. We were enjoying the weather, so our kitchen became quite elaborate. The digging became a kind of primitive architecture that allowed us to establish a feeling of home in this cold, white, isolated environment. We carved benches in the side of the pit where we could sit to prepare food and eat. We also carved a work area in the opposite side of the snow pit, including a shelf set aside for stoves. No open water runs in a place like Mount Logan, so we were required to melt snow for cooking, drinking, and cleaning. We spent an extraordinary amount of time melting snow. Taking the time to build this kitchen area correctly shaped the social center of our camp, a reminder that everything you dig up, everything you carve, becomes the space that defines you.

When we went to bed that night we were also reminded of the other qualities of a snow cave. They are warm, so it is challenging to stay dry. They are completely dark and silent. I wiped a drop of water from my forehead, calmed my spirit, and began to think of tomorrow. Prayer begins with silence.

The standard route up Mount Logan is not technically difficult. It is called King's Trench. It does require glacier travel skills, which include crevasse rescue. These are lessons learned over years in the mountains. To come to a place like Logan without confidence in your abilities on ice, glaciers, and snow would be to put everyone's lives at risk. You must travel with flagged wands, ropes, ascending devices, snow picks, snow saws, ice axes, a sense of adventure, and great patience. Only the rare climber is gifted with patience. It is not unusual to die without it.

Glacier travel is slow. One must remember that a glacier is a river of ice, always, invisibly on the move, leaving cracks in its wake. The crevasses on Mount Logan are massive in size. Imagine large buildings being swallowed into their frozen, blue belly. Imagine one of us disappearing into the mountain's icy gut, which could happen even more easily. That being said, these large, threatening crevasses are not the ones that create the greatest anxiety. Many more, quite capable of gobbling us up, are invisible, covered with snow. Safety dictates a patterned method of traveling on these glaciers. Tedious, exhausting, and slow, this pattern can become a matter of life or death.

We reviewed our safety standards. Early in the day they seemed perfectly reasonable. We moved up the glacier with Bob in the lead. He probed with his ice axe. What was beneath us? On Mount Logan, it could have been an ice pack centuries old, or it could have been the place where the river of ice shifted and left a void hungry for a careless climber. As each spot was deemed safe, a wand was placed as a marker. Standard operating procedure required that we place a wand about every 100 feet. A climbing rope is either 150 or 165 feet in length and takes approximately six feet of rope to tie off each climber. Sometimes there are three climbers on one rope. The idea is that if you are following the rope up or down the mountain, there will be at least one wand for each rope length. Occasionally, someone will probe, and their axe will break through the snow into open air. It's time to check your rope and carefully find a way around the hidden crevasse. Everyone must share the commitment to do this correctly. If properly done, this marking of your route provides a safe passageway up and down the glacier.

Each glacier is crossed many times. The mountain is far too big to climb in a day, so we intended to establish camps a day's travel up and down the mountain. These camps were much like our base camp. The same attention was given to safety, while a little less was given to the elaborate comfort provided by snowy architectural designs. On the way up we carried heavy loads of food, climbing tools, and camping gear. We crossed the glacier on skis. These skis had a free heel so you could walk in them. They also had removable adhesive on the bottom referred to as climbing skins. The material of the skins only slides one way so that you can ski up a quite steep slope without sliding backwards. While the ascent was hard and slow, there was much joy on the way back down. We removed the skins, hoisted our now near-empty packs, and embraced the freedom to ski fast and free. Fast and free, as long as we stayed on the route we had correctly marked the first time we skied the glacier.

For our first climb up the glacier, we all filled our packs with as many bamboo wands as possible. Hundreds of these wands would be placed on our route. They allowed us to see our route and to know that it was safe. I swung my pack onto my back, grabbed my ice axe, and found myself excited about the tedium that lay ahead.

Bob and Dave were the ones who insisted on doing everything correctly. As Will stood in line, watching Bob probe and then carefully place wand after wand, he became impatient. He was in a hurry and was occasionally willing to compromise the details of safety so that we could speed our progress. I didn't know George, and I was convinced that I was the one with the well-adjusted sense of balance.

But of course, everyone believed that of themselves.

As the day continued, our backs became tired and we became anxious for Mount Logan to reveal more of her secrets. The gentle weather lulled us into lethargy, and we began to think, "A wand every rope length is a lot. Perhaps every two or even three rope lengths would be enough. It seems like we can see forever!" This made immediate sense to Will. Standing around with cold feet and wanting to move, I bought into it quickly. It took three days of marking glaciers before it was time to begin to move our equipment higher. This first, safe journey to the location of our next camp took about ten hours. We skied down in less than one hour. After ascending together, we enjoyed the freedom of skiing down alone.

Late in the afternoon of the third day, Will and I descended to base camp earlier than the others. As they drifted in, we began to prepare the evening meal. The tedium of a climbing adventure continued as we melted snow for cooking as well as enough for all five us to stay hydrated through the night and all day tomorrow. Dave skied in and then George. It seemed odd that Bob was this far behind the others, but it was not unusual for him

24

to want some time alone. After about forty-five minutes, Will said, "Look up on the glacier. Is Bob walking? Where are his skis?" I took out my binoculars and scanned the slopes above. Bob was walking. He looked okay, so we turned to complete our chores. When he walked into camp he seemed frustrated as he threw his pack to the ground in a rough and unaccustomed fashion.

"Did you cook for me?" he asked.

"Of course," I said. "You okay?"

"We'll talk about it later. After you eat, will you get your climbing gear together and head back up the glacier with me?"

"Sure," I said. I was the person in the group with the most rescue experience. Usually when ropes and safety systems were required, the others deferred to me.

Everyone left him to his silence. Bob was the most experienced and strongest climber among us. He was universally respected, and while not gruff, he was known to appreciate some private space from time to time. In some ways, each of us was like that. After we finished eating, I shouldered my pack filled with climbing gear, and Bob and I headed back up the glacier in the evening sun. We were silent as we moved. It was obvious something had happened to his skis and we were going to find them. Bob would tell me what happened when he was ready, and that would be soon enough.

As we settled into a rhythm, Bob began to offer his story in small bits and pieces. Our skis had a safety strap that was buckled around the ankle. That way if the ski should break loose from the binding it would still be attached to your leg. Bob forgot to fasten his. As he was skiing a fast and free descent he caught an edge, his ski popped off, and went flying into a deep, wide crevasse. It seemed that even the most safety-conscious among us could be careless. This was an important reminder early in the trip. Later, this kind of carelessness could cost someone their life.

As we stared at the lip of an imposing crevasse, the bright white light of snow disappeared into a vacant darkness. We could only imagine what was below. Not knowing where the ski landed, we knew someone had to descend into the icy depths of the crevasse to find it. Bob would go, and it would be my job to catch him if a snowy ledge broke or if he simply fell.

The safety standard requires three points of contact. This may seem excessive, but you must remember that your companion's life is on the other end of the rope. I used two dead men, the slang term for an aluminum V-shaped wedge, and a snow picket, which is a longer, thinner, four-foot-long narrow aluminum wedge. I drove them into the snow at forty-five-degree angles, in an arch behind me, strung tubular nylon webbing between them, and attached my climbing harness to the webbing with two locking carabiners, each opening gate turned in a different direction. I hooked a descending device into the beaner in the front of my harness. This would be used to slow the pull of the rope if Bob should fall. He tied in to the other end of the rope and slowly descended an icy ramp into the crevasse as I let out just enough rope to give him the freedom to move. There was no way to know if the ramp was stable or not.

One of the things inherent in mountaineering is the constant awareness that you are placing your life in the hands of someone else. While this may seem difficult, it can be more difficult to consider another placing their life in your hands. One of the keys to managing this well is to know when to think about it and when to banish it from your imagination. As you train and learn rope systems you constantly remember, "Someone may live or die depending on my ability to get this right. Someone's family may or may not have a mother or father if I become lazy and quit paying attention to detail." It is a constant and critical thought. When you are on the mountain, moving, roped up to your partner who is descending over the lip of a crevice, tied into the person on the other end of the rope whom you can no longer see—at that moment there are many more important demands on your thoughts. Proper ice-axe placement, not outrunning your rope, being sure you do not go somewhere from which you cannot return. At this point you either trust your partner and yourself or you don't. If you don't, you should not be there. Go home.

Bob descended uneventfully. His ski was easy to reach, but of course I didn't know that since he was concealed in the dark, mysterious world of the crevasse. He tugged on the rope, giving me the signal that he was coming back up. It is important to keep the rope taut so that you can catch someone if they fall. Gradually I saw his shadow emerge as he moved into the light, the sun at his back. As he climbed back out we were careful, not surrendering to the temptation of hurried carelessness. I coiled the rope correctly and did not relax until he stood before me. The whole event was pretty simple, but they always seem simple when everything works. If the most safety conscious among us can make an error this severe, this early in the trip, we must become hyper-vigilant as the days wear on and altitude and exhaustion begin to take their toll.

Higher on the mountain the route is steeper and crevasse danger is dramatically diminished. This doesn't mean travel is faster, or safer, just different. By this point our packs were heavy as we carried gear to establish three new camps. We were at a much higher altitude and oxygen was in short supply. We were excited. Everyone wanted to carry the heaviest load possible so we would have to make fewer trips.

We protected our eyes with goggles as we faced the brilliant sun and the clear blue sky. There was no need for the sunscreen we brought, so it stayed in our packs. The air was so cold that no flesh could be exposed to the sun. We wore several layers of clothing and were constantly opening and closing zippers, adding and removing caps and layered gloves so that we could manage temperature and sweat. Our skis were the safest way to travel. Skis distribute your weight over a broader area and make it less likely that you will break through the snow into an unmarked crevasse. We headed up, with sixty-pound packs, at altitude, gasping for breath. On the way, up skis were safe but not fast. Everyone looked forward to the evening descent. We checked our bindings to be sure they were correctly attached to our boots and tugged the safety strap that encircled our ankles. No one mentioned Bob's earlier error as we anticipated the sound of our skis slicing rapidly through the snow. Following the well-marked route back to base camp was thrilling. Tomorrow we would get up and do it again.

The next day, late in the morning, I received an unwelcome surprise. I had been following our carefully marked path, moving gear up to the next camp. One foot in front of the other. Stop every few steps to breathe the thin air and then, chest pain. At first I thought it was no big deal. In these circumstances, everyone hurts. This was different. It was a stabbing pain in the center of my chest that was not there yesterday. I took a break and it went away. As I started to climb again I looked at my watch. Nine minutes and there it was again. If the discomfort is just exhaustion, rest will provide recovery. If it repeats, the chances build that it is cardiac related. I stopped, the pain receded; I climbed, nine minutes and the pain returned. I followed this pattern several more times. As we headed toward our higher camp on the safely marked route, everyone moved at their own pace. We joyfully embraced the isolation. As I began to evaluate my situation, I needed solitude. I did not want to talk about this unwelcome intrusion.

My anxiety rose, but I knew I could not surrender to its subtle demand for control. I was not having a heart attack. Breathe deep and do what you have to do. Here, success or failure is not a personal issue. It matters to everyone. We had spent all year training, saving money, and negotiating with our families and jobs for a month away from home. We had spent a lifetime developing egos that told us we were good enough to succeed on a mountain like Logan. When I stopped, my pack slid easily off my back. I used it for a bench, ate a snack, and tried to consider my options. There weren't many. I could ignore it. I would probably be okay. It did not take long to reject this option. Ignoring these symptoms would put everyone at risk. We had put our lives in each other's hands. What were they supposed to do with me if I had a heart attack at 18,000 feet, in a storm on Mount Logan? These were not the kind of men who would leave me. Streaky, cirrus clouds had been moving across the sky all day. In their wake the heavens were turning the kind of dark blue that indicates a storm. I shoved a mouthful of Ann's fruitcake in my mouth. It was rich in calories and it did not harden in the cold. I washed it down with tea from my thermos and realized that it was time to move. Shouldering my pack I climbed to the next camp. There, with the storm looming on the horizon, I told Bob, Will, and George the news. There was not much discussion. I didn't ask them what they thought, I just announced, "If I stay here, I'll probably be alright, but I'll put everyone in danger. I'm going to go back down and fly out."

Anger, discouragement, and even shame began to cloud my thinking. Was I not good enough to be in a place like this? Had I wasted the time

29

and energy these guys put into this trip? I could not see clearly into the cloudy place in my heart, and as I looked up I realized I could not see clearly at all. The sky had become one thick, impenetrable blanket of falling snow. I am an emotional person and expected to be emotional about this, but one's priorities take strange twists in a place like Logan. We didn't have time to surrender to feelings. It was understood that I must descend right now or we could be stuck in this camp for several days. This was no time to think about anything but how to travel in a storm. Having all agreed that my presence would compromise the group's safety, we decided I should return to base camp. It was too complicated for five people to descend safely through the storm. Two was enough. Dave simply said, "I'll go," and we prepared to ski off together. Dave could ascend our marked route alone after the storm. Our pilot provided a safety flyover every few days. Perhaps I would be able to signal him after the storm passed and get a flight out. We jettisoned all extra gear. There was plenty of food and fuel at base camp. We picked up our light packs, skis, ropes, and crevasse rescue equipment and were ready to go. A simple 'See you later' sent us on our way. The snow was becoming heavier, and it was difficult to see. If I had thought the decision to return was hard, I had no idea of the test we would face in returning.

This was the point where it became clear why the wands must be so close together. We could not see. I reached up to clean the snow off my goggles. Removing them, I wiped away the snow, put them back on, yet I still could see nothing. The world was white. There was no discernible distinction between heaven and earth. We could not tell up from down, north from south. It was snowing so hard that our skis did not move downhill. We were directionless. It was time to put our skills to work. There were markers to be found.

Despite the risks, we knew how to do this. We had done it before. We took the time to review procedure. This was going to be our life for many hours. It was important to get it right. This was that time when it was not helpful to think about the two of us placing our lives in each other's hands. There were no other good choices. We either believed in each other or we didn't. It was far too late to think of such things. The decision to trust was made long ago.

First, we put on our climbing harnesses and tied in using the most basic of climbing knots, the figure eight. With Dave and me roped together, if I, the lead skier, fell through the snow into a crevasse, he would be able to catch me without being dragged in on top of me. Dave took two dead men and placed them at 45-degree angles, several feet apart. We acknowledged that the standard was three points of contact, but we only had two easily at hand. While we could bury a pack for the third one, we were preparing to do this hundreds of times. That would extend our descent for hours, perhaps another day. We decided that trusting the placement of two dead men was a better compromise than extended exposure to the storm. We kept the rope taut, only letting out enough for me to slowly ski toward the invisible wands. I could not see the next wand. I knew its tip was no longer six feet above the snow. In this storm it might now show a mere four feet above the snow pack, and by tomorrow it could be buried.

Trust your preparation.

There is a wand, less than a rope length away. Then another, then another. I ski back and forth in a slow-moving arc until I reach the next wand. When I get there I tug on the rope and slowly pull Dave as he skis directly to me. We do this again and again and again. There is no anxiety. I have no memory of whether the chest pains continued at this point. We know what to do and how to do it and think of nothing else. Years of training provide the confidence that leads us wand to wand through the whiteout. The experience of peace, even in this crisis, overwhelms me.

We had encouraged Bob to compromise, spread the wands out, we had said. He had refused. That is why we have a path in the storm, it is why are safe now. As Dave follows the rope and skis beside me we continue, one step at a time, don't stop. Although the storm and its cloud cover warm the air considerably, it remains very cold. Don't check the temperature; it doesn't matter. It's too cold to stand around and wait, no time to think. The snow and the cold are dangerous and we are a long way from escaping either of them. We keep moving in the dim light. The wind howls so loudly that we cannot hear each other talk. Even our shouts are lost in the storm. We search for the markers; these wands exist to show us the way.

In the fourteenth chapter of the Gospel of John, Jesus promised his disciples peace. It seemed to be a strange promise in their circumstance. Jesus's intimate friends accepted the notion that he would not grow old and die a natural death, but that he was likely to die a violent death at the hands of the occupying forces of Rome or even at the hands of their own religious leaders. The imminence of his death became the vision that dominated their collective imagination. They were imagining correctly. He would be crucified by the end of the week. It was in this swirling storm of fearful anticipation that Jesus said:

"Peace I leave with you; my peace I give to you. I do not give to you as the world gives. Do not let your hearts be troubled, and do not let them be afraid." (John 14:27 NRSV)

When Jesus said this, I imagine his friends looking at him in bewildered wonder and thinking that he was going to die and they might be killed with him. Where is the peace in that?

We sometimes embrace the illusion that a vigorous and vital faith in God will remove all of the obstacles to peace from our lives. This is no one's experience. Not even Jesus's. His story seems to point in a radically different direction. On the night that he offers this promise, he also provides markers that point the way to maintaining this peace.

"Love one another in the same way I have loved you." (John 13:35)

"I will not leave you orphaned." (John 14:18)

"I have told you this before it occurs so that when it does occur, you may believe." (John 14:29)

Certainly Jesus's followers are not the first or last to rope up in a storm and wonder if they could find the markers leading to a safe passage or if this was the storm that represented the death of peace in their lives. While people of faith may see death as the ultimate experience of peace, the road we travel to get there can be quite harrowing. The crevasses that would freeze the life out of us are a hidden danger, yet we do not have to allow them to dominate our lives or fashion our spirits in fear. As we peer into the storm, we are tethered to a faithful companion who will not abandon us when we lose our way. By taking the time to chart the path that will lead us through the storms before they arrive, we can be assured that our pathway to peace is well marked and can be found. And we keep moving.

If you repeat anything long enough it can become rote: a mantra of action. We descend for hours when it becomes clear that I have been skiing far too long without having found a wand. I come to the end of the rope and realize that I must have passed one by now, turned too far to one side or another. I am going the wrong way. If I ski past our invisible, snow-covered camp, there will be no way to return and find it. Turning in the direction I think is uphill, I resume skiing. How will I let Dave know I am coming his way? His knowing is essential, so that he will gather the slack in the rope. Instead I pull on the rope and he gives me extra slack, just as he is supposed to do, and just as I hope he will not. I don't know what else to do except ski in the direction I think will lead me back to him; a slack rope does not provide the safety or confidence of a taut line. This is an absolute stab in the dark, or perhaps I should say a stab in the white.

By this time my hands and feet are numb with cold. I cannot feel and cannot see well. I am dependent on my partner, a rope, and the wands. We have been dependent on each other before. I maintain complete confidence in him. As the rope begins to gather behind my uphill journey, I see it move. Somehow he has intuited what is happening and he pulls in the slack rope. He also takes a few wands out of his pack and marks the direction from which I am returning so that I will not make the same mistake again. When I see him emerge on the snowy horizon we slap each other on the back but do not try to speak as I immediately turn around and ski off into the storm. We cannot stop. I have to find our next wand. It is snowing so hard that soon they will not stick out above the snow pack.

I seek a sweet spot where arousal, fueled by adrenaline, stress, and muscle memory, kicks in to open our imaginations, leading us to new levels of confidence. This sweet spot is beyond knowing, beyond thinking or feeling. We step into it and simply exist. Our bodies know what to do and how to do it. This is an internal gift born of surrender. No longer trying to control our environment, not wishing for what is not there, abandoning the hope of clear skies, we simply are. We were in that spot.

Out of the dim light, another slim wand points to the almost invisible sky. I find a wand, then another, then another. There are hours of wands to follow. We do. Again and again. Suddenly they stop. There are no more. Are they finally buried in fresh snow? Have we somehow gotten off course? I look around and then probe with my ski poles until I detect hardened piles of ice that break off into deep soft pits of fresh snow; our cooking pit, and finally the entrance to our snow caves, evidence that we are in base camp. We clear the entrances of snow and crawl into these rooms that promise sleep. As we take off our boots and bury ourselves deeply into our sleeping bags, I experience a sense of relief. As the tension drains out of my mind and body, the threat of anxiety knocks at the door. What will tomorrow bring? The purity and simplicity of following wands through a storm has past. The first hints of the depth of disappointment lurk like shadows on the snow. At that moment I decide that I cannot indulge the urge to slide into darkness. There are still important decisions to be made. I know myself well enough to know that a harsh depression waits for me at home. It will have to wait.

At this moment, we fall at last into sleep, wrapped in an exhausted cocoon of physical peace. We are grateful that we had several bright sunny days to place markers along the way. Grateful that we had placed them often enough. Grateful that on a beautiful day with gentle weather, we imagined the possibility of life at the bottom of a crevasse, or wandering across Mount Logan's vast ice fields unable to find our camp. We were grateful for Bob's insistence on the orthodoxy of safety procedures. Mostly we are grateful for the promise of several hours of blissful, warm, dry, windless sleep.

It's difficult to think of the requirements of safety in a storm on a day with calm weather. On the day the storm roars in, it's difficult to think of anything else. Whatever the world is like today may change tomorrow. Bob's insistence on providing a clear way provided a path that kept us safe. There had been those markers in place to help me find my way. Adventures like this are an important part of my life, but they are not my life. At home Ann and our kids are waiting for me. I have a meaningful job and a deep faith, all of which represent a life of purpose. I work hard to secure these things. They are not at risk. The cave provides an environment insulated from the storm. Warm and silent, I exist completely in the moment. I wipe a drop of water from my forehead.

Prayer begins with silence.

The next morning the storm abated. We are outside of the warm cocoon of our cave. Our sputtering stove melts snow for tea and soup. The whine of a small plane interrupts our silence before we can see it. We look to the sky and soon he appears. The world is smooth and white, so our pilot is able to recognize the disrupted snow and our brightly colored skis as erect as wands in our base camp. It doesn't seem right to him, so he lands to take a look. On that day he is flying a Cessna 185, the preferred plane of many bush pilots. It is much more nimble than the Beaver that brought us here. The 185 can take off quickly and is able to carry an unusually heavy load for such a small plane. Today's load carries the weight of a heavy heart and not much else. I assure him that there is no immediate danger, but that I am no longer a useful member of this climbing team. Paul and I fly away. We circle a few times and watch as Dave begins to ski back up the glacier to join the others. It is a clear day. Dave easily follows the wands that mark the way of safety. There will be many more days where I will search for markers to offer clarity in life's moments of uncertainty and fear. Many moments when they will clarify the pathway to peace.

The Way My Uncles Taught Me

I'm no carpenter. Well into my second year as a rural Alaskan pastor, contractor, and construction worker, I remained the essence of unskilled labor. If a carpenter built a pattern, I could copy it, but I had to be shown time and time again how to lay out the pattern for framing walls, and retaught how to build headers and footers for windows and doors. While I was learning these things, I worked more slowly than others. I worked alone, late into the night, trying to complete the days' assignments before it was time to start again. Our head carpenter, Mac, liked to say, "The last preacher who was a good carpenter was Jesus, and we never saw his work, so we can't be sure." I took some small comfort in that.

The carpentry skills were applied, for good or ill, to a church. Despite my limited skill as a carpenter, I had become a convincing recruiter, beginning most mornings on the phone persuading folks to spend their day off building the North Star United Methodist Church in Nikiski, Alaska. This small congregation of about twenty people and friends were now nearing the final stages of construction, having built the church from the ground up. We did it all, from surveying our uncleared seven-acre lot to building the altar for the soon-to-be completed sanctuary. We cut every board and drove every nail as an act of devotion, volunteerism, and love. Having managed to frame and enclose the building during Alaska's short construction season, we were now hoping to finish the interior by Easter Sunday. Remaining were countless small chores and one big one, the installation of the boiler, a complicated and hugely important task in Alaska! We had until Sunday morning. Today, it was Wednesday.

With the clock ticking, I sat alone in anxious silence and waited. Among all the things I do well, I do these poorly: waiting, silence. My good friend, the master of many trades, Nic Sacaloff had said he would take care of the boiler, and I was to be his assistant. He had assured me, "I'll be there first thing in the morning, Pastor Billy. We have time to get this done."

It was one o'clock in the afternoon. I had not heard from Nic. Few places are ever fully silent, certainly not our spot on the North Road on Alaska's Kenai Peninsula. I heard trucks drive by, planes fly over, birds chirping, snowplows pushing snow, but I did not hear the one thing my heart was aching to recognize, the weight of Nic's truck, crushing gravel and ice as he was driving up to the work site. I had been looking forward to being his assistant all week. Working with him was great pleasure. His quiet, non-anxious presence was a balm to my noisy, cluttered, anxiety-ridden soul. Me, the master of 'What if' thoughts:

What if he doesn't come?
What if it's not done by Easter?
What if everyone is discouraged?
What if they finally realize that I am in over my head and don't know what I'm doing?
What if...what if...what if...

While I imagined Nic spending the morning in his perpetual calm, I had been jittery. I moved constantly from the front steps to the boiler room, as if my presence in either place would telepathically call him. Stare at the driveway and Nic will appear. Stare at the boiler and it will produce hot water.

Hours later, in the early afternoon, he showed up to install the boiler. He offered no explanation. He just appeared. I wondered where he had been, why he was so late. After working as his assistant for a few hours I could hold my curiosity at bay no longer. I wanted him to share my anxiety.

"Nic, where have you been all morning? We got a really late start."

"I was home praying, Pastor Billy. I got a job call and I was late because I was deciding what to do."

Nic was a contract worker on an offshore oil platform. Since he did not work for the oil company, his shifts were never guaranteed. When he got a call, it was important for him to go. Nic and his wife Vita needed the money, and if he said no the company just called someone else. That morning he had gotten a call. He and Vita spent the next few hours praying about what to do. Go to the platform or install the boiler. Going to the platform promised money to pay the bills. Installing the boiler promised that the community's first worship service in the new church would be on Easter Sunday.

Although it was not Nic's intent, I felt embarrassed. Why had I spoken? Why had I not trusted him to come? Why had I not just been grateful that he was here now? Far too often, I speak first and think later. At least, I could be really glad I hadn't called.

Frequently I stand in front of the church and say, "Prayer begins with silence." Someone always challenges me. They eagerly wait for me after the service to lodge their complaint.

"What about a crisis?" they protest. When I look up and see I am going to be hit by a car I don't have time for silence. I just want to pray. I want to pray like this, "OH GOD, HELP ME!!"

I never argue. I concede their point. They are correct. Prayer can seem quite natural when faced with a car wreck, unexpected bad news, or any number of immediate crises…so let me say, minus that car running the red light and the sound of shattered glass announcing imminent disaster, "Prayer begins with silence."

When I think of prayer beginning with silence, I think of prayer as responsive speech. It begins with God and then I respond. Silence provides the context for praying. God speaks out of the silence and then perhaps I have something to say.

In Gracias! A Latin American Journal, Henri Nouwen describes the silence with which he begins his day. "Every morning at 6:45 I go to the small convent of the Carmelite Sisters for an hour of prayer and meditation. I say every morning, but there are exceptions. Fatigue, busyness, and preoccupation often serve as arguments for not going. Yet without this one-hour-a-day for God, my life loses its coherency. I start experiencing my days as a series of random incidents and accidents."

Nouwen goes on to say that this time is not generally a time of deep insight, or one where he feels especially close to God. To him this often feels like useless time. However, he believed that it was this useless time, this one-hour of silence, that held his life together. This time of silence provided a context for his day, which shielded him from self-importance. Much like a small Sabbath, it insured that the world and all its business could continue without him.

Everyone carried on just fine as he sat in silence and listened. Then, when he got up to engage the world, he engaged with a different kind of thoughtful humility.

The importance of silence is a life principle that I did not learn as a child. I grew up in a loud, joyful Southern home filled with hospitality, family, guests, food, and very little silence. We looked out the window often as our eyes scanned the street in anticipation of our arriving guests. My mother even baked cookies so she could greet the young Mormon missionaries who wandered our neighborhood in a vain search for converts. To this day, I imagine the smell of my great aunts' powder lingering on the collar of my shirt, the residue of their greeting and embrace. We were taught to be gracious hosts, vigorous storytellers, and creative cooks confidently entertaining our guests while seeing to their every need.

This uninterrupted and entertaining form of hospitality did not always serve me well when my wife Ann and our two-year-old son, Chris moved to Nikiski, Alaska, where I was the pastor of the North Star United Methodist Church. Our parish consisted of two trailers on an uncleared lot, one to live in and one for worship. We lived in a house trailer that was tiny, fifty by twelve feet. In the winter the windows were covered with ice on the inside as well as the outside. As the frost would rise up on the door, it was a good indicator of the temperature outside. This was in the early 1980s, long before cable TV arrived in rural Alaska. The internet was not even a dream. We had a small portable TV on a stand across from the sleeper sofa. You had to remove the TV and its stand when you opened the sofa. There was not room for both of them. This didn't matter much. We had TV reception less than half the time and when we did, it was on a two-week delay. It did not seem odd to us that The Charlie Brown Christmas Special was viewed in mid-January.

When we arrived in Nikiski, about twenty hopeful people were associated with the North Star United Methodist Church. Among them were Nic and Vita Sacaloff. Nic and Vita were some of the first people to befriend us in Nikiski. Nic was often called away from home to work on the offshore oil platform in the Cook Inlet. Vita worked to maintain their home and to care for the many relatives who stayed there from time to time. Nic was one of the people known as Dena'ina. There are only two small reservations in Alaska. The Dena'ina of the Kenai Peninsula did not live on one of them. The land claims of all other indigenous people were settled through the Alaska Native Land Claims Settlement Act. Vita was not Dena'ina, though she lived as if she were. She joined Nic in providing an open door, food, and lodging to any family member who arrived and asked for hospitality. They fed all of these folks with the food they harvested on the Kenai Peninsula. Each September, during the hunting season, Nic would kill a moose and they would process it for winter food. The law allowed one moose per person. If they needed two moose, then he would help another family member harvest theirs. A common greeting in September on the Kenai would be, "Have you got your moose?"

They also fished for salmon. Native people were allowed by law to harvest more fish in more varied ways than recent immigrants like me. They could fish subsistence off the beach with gill nets, while we were restricted to fishing with poles and artificial bait. Subsistence harvest meant that they could catch fish in the traditional manner for feeding their extended families. Their legal limits were much higher than ours. Salmon fishing in the Cook Inlet is defined by the movement of the tides. As the tide comes in, the fish arrive with it. They move parallel to the beach and head for the freshwater streams from which they came. Restricted by fish and game regulations from using a net or live bait, I would cast my brightly colored fishing lure into the dark, fast-moving water and hope for a miracle. Possession limits change from day to day, and I would listen to the fish and game report on the radio for up-to-date information. Most often I could harvest three salmon a day and have a possession limit of six fish. This means that on the day of a late-night high tide, I could go out after we put the kids to bed, catch three fish, wait until midnight, and then catch three more. At the same time, our native friends would place their gill nets in the water from the beach, capturing large numbers of fish as they followed the shoreline headed for freshwater streams. Ann, our young son Chris, and I were often invited to sit around the bonfire on the beach and join in the wait for high tide.

There were no restrictions on berry picking. Everyone was invited to pick berries to make jelly and preserves to add variety to our diet. Blackberries, blueberries, salmon berries, raspberries all grew rapidly in a land with long, cool days. Harvesting food in this way was a joyful, social, community activity that guaranteed a multigenerational summer. In addition to this work, there was a house to maintain. The season for home repair was short. Snow remains into May and the ground is frozen even longer. It snows again in early October. Once it snows, the time for home repairs is over. Along with many others, Nic and Vita spent at least half of his onshore time working at the church. None of this was easy. Knowing how hard they worked added a layer of meaning to their friendship.

As they joined others in the congregation in providing our first introduction to indigenous people, they also provided our first introduction to social silence. Nic's uncle, Peter Kalifornsky, and his mother, Feodosia Sacaloff, were the last two people who were fluent in the Dena'ina language. Nic spoke Dena'ina as a child, but for many years English had been his spoken language. As they changed their spoken language, one thing that didn't change was the speech and social patterns of the Dena'ina people. This is what happened.

Nic would call me on the phone and say, "Pastor Billy, this is Nic (long pause)." The silence felt awkward to me. It was more than my Southern heritage would allow. I would leap into the void, begin to talk and Nic would remain silent.

Finally, after I had chattered myself out of ideas he would say, "Maybe Vita and I will come over for a visit."

"Sure," I would say. "Come on over."

Nic and Vita would then come to our home for a visit. When they arrived at our trailer, we would invite them in and offer them a cup of tea. Nic was a short man, about five feet six inches tall with dark brown skin and thick black hair that hung down, shading his eyes. Vita was a bit taller, thin, and her face was graced with a continual smile. They were lovely people with the contented rugged look of those who worked hard. When we took each other's hands in greeting theirs were cut, callused, and scarred. Ours were soft and easily blistered.

Once we invited them inside they were content to sit in silence, comfortable sharing our space as we went about our business. Perhaps they would pick up a magazine or perhaps they would just sip tea and relax. Feeling obligated to entertain, I drilled them with questions and overwhelmed them with stories until I ran out of energy. Finally, I would join them in their silence, yet it felt rude to me, as if I were no longer a good host. After a couple of hours, they would stand and say their goodbyes. Thanking us for the tea and our friendship, they would be on their way.

Ann and I were baffled, having no understanding of the social customs that were being observed. Sometimes Nic and Vita invited us to their house. It was the same, tea and silence. It took me a long time and some wise counselors before I began to understand that they felt blessed when we shared each other's company. No need to entertain. We could simply be together. We could simply be.

Nic was a leader in our church. He was smart, hardworking, and wise. It surprised me when he knocked on the door of our trailer one day to say that he wanted to resign from the Board of Trustees, where he was a valued member. "Nic, why do you want to resign?" I asked. "You make a huge contribution."

"I don't think so," Nic said. "I never finish a sentence."

When I asked what that meant, Nic explained to me that the Dena'ina people were part of a larger cultural group of Athabaskan people. Their speech and cultural patterns were quite different from ours. It was considered kind for them to share home visits in silence. It was considered rude to talk all the time.

Their speech patterns differed from ours, too. Dena'ina speakers, even when they speak English, have long pauses between phrases. Folks from outside of this culture often become uncomfortable with the silence and jump in, trying to finish sentences and thoughts for our native friends. We have a tendency to interpret their silence as a lack of confidence or even intelligence. Often we think they are slow; they think we are rude. Nic told me that he never was allowed to complete a thought in the trustee meetings. Someone jumped into the silence to speak for him. More often than not, the words they choose were not the ones waiting in Nic's heart and mind.

"Nic, I would like to ask you not to resign. What if we had a meeting where you taught us about your speech patterns, where they come from, and why they are important? You could teach us how to practice being quiet until you finish speaking. Often I fill in the silence with the mistaken idea that I am being helpful."

Nic smiled. "It doesn't seem helpful," he said.

The next time the Board of Trustees met, Nic was responsible for the agenda. He spoke with us about the significance of letting someone finish, of the value of silence, and the respect offered by slowing down. This was not easy for us to hear. During the first half of the meeting we often interrupted with, "Yeah, but." It was difficult for us not to feel criticized or even accused. When one of us would interrupt the silence with an anxious suggestion that we may not finish in time, Nic just smiled and waited. He let our impatience speak for itself.

Later, Nic told me how silence had been his teacher as a child. Much of his childhood had been spent across the Cook Inlet in the small, remote village of New Tyonek, hundreds of miles from a road. He spent most of his time there with his uncles. They were the last people known to hunt beluga whales from Baidarkas, one-or two-holed kayaks made from sealskin. Imagine paddling up to a huge white, toothed whale rising from the ocean depths while you raise a handheld harpoon and thrust it into the whale's side. The people believed the whale decided to offer itself to them as a gift. To believe otherwise would have displayed an overwhelming arrogance. As Nic's uncles built these boats, he would watch and then it would be his turn. He stitched the sealskin cover onto the frame made of willow and bone, while they watched carefully and without comment. When he got to a resting place, one of them would speak like this:

"That's an interesting way to do it. My grandfather did it this way." Then he would take over and work on the boat while Nic watched.

They repeated this pattern over and over until finally the boat was finished carefully and correctly. Nic told me that his uncles never corrected him, never scolded him, never told him he was wrong. They simply took turns watching each other and offering alternative ways to work. Their silence provided a welcoming environment for their instruction. While I would have insisted upon verbal instruction to be sure everyone got it right, they were content to accept that this may simply take a lot more time. This kind of teaching provided lessons likely to last a lifetime.

While our family lived in Nikiski, Nic's uncle and mother died, and along with them the spoken language known as Dena'ina. While their language is recorded in writing, that is an academic exercise. It is effectively gone from the daily life of the people. The unnamed voices of their ancestors are being lost along with their language. Their culture survives by the thinnest of threads, hanging on against the intrusion of the larger world.

Nic and Vita invite us to spend an afternoon in their home. We walk up the stairs, through the arctic entryway and into the warm quiet. Their dog silently approaches to sniff and offer his approval. Vita offers us a seat in the living room and a cup of tea. We exchange greetings as they go about their daily business. The conversation includes pauses that are far too long for my comfort. I continually interrupt the silence with questions and observations. They are exceptionally kind as they tolerate my incessant speech. I realize what I have done and pick up a magazine off the coffee table. They generously accept my mishandled intentions while displaying no need to talk about it. I wonder how much of life I have simply talked over.

The primary thing Nic taught me was that our silence provides a context for our speaking. He taught me that it wasn't necessary to talk just to fill the void. We could be together, observing how others go about their business without judging. We could begin to understand where they needed help and where they didn't, what they found interesting and what was tiresome to them. When we allowed the other one to finish a thought, we learned from them without competition or argument. Then when we spoke, our words would hold a depth of meaning that could not be contained in hurried small talk.

The Bible recognizes this need for silence as a foundational principle of creation. It teaches us a rhythm of life that allows for extended periods of quiet. This is known as Sabbath keeping. While Sabbath keeping does not require complete silence, it does provide a platform for extended separation from the intensity of our daily lives. This allows us to create a different context for our relationship with God and others. As I stand in a culture of busyness, I become deeply resistant to this way of being.

When I live as if this is true, I experience a deep creativity, a new kind of peace. This quiet day, different from other days, contains this peaceful promise. As I learn to live this way I practice particular principles of Sabbath keeping. For me the heart of the matter is being available to God. I do not speak because I have nothing to say. I listen, not knowing what I am listening for. Often when I speak my prayers, I find myself directing God. "God, it would be nice if you would do this or that." I want to discover an agenda larger than my own. From the very beginning I confess that I don't know what it is.

49

I keep the Sabbath on Friday. I am a pastor and while I love Sunday, it usually involves three worship services and another event or two. It is not restful. So on Thursday night and Friday, I remember the Sabbath day and keep it holy.

I begin in the evening: We sit for our evening meal with those who are important to us and close at hand. This beginning is different from the way most Americans understand the rhythm of the day, and it offers an important distinction. Instead of waking filled with anxiety for all I must accomplish, I wake in the morning and find that the Sabbath is well underway. Half of it is past. I have accomplished nothing measurable, and everything is okay. The world continues to move along just fine. This is a revelation to me. Could it be that my presence, while important, beautiful and God-alive, is not essential every moment?

I spend much of the day alone. I run or ride my bicycle. I enjoy training for ultramarathons. Each year I run two or three trail races that are fifty miles long. This requires a long training run each week. These runs are how I spend most Friday mornings. Depending on where I am in my training cycle, I run two to six hours. Angie is my colleague at work and my primary training partner. Sometimes we go on our long run together. When we do, we agree not to speak for the first half of the run. Because it is early in the morning and we are silent, there are many things to observe. Often we see deer, and in the summer we find that the trails of the Sonoran desert are alive. We do not look for snakes. Instead we look for things that seem out of place: a design that is too patterned, a rock that is too round or in the wrong place. By observing in this manner, we not only see snakes but the occasional roadrunner, desert tortoise, gila monster, lizards, rabbits, the infrequent sleeping javelina, deer, and on the rarest occasion, a mountain lion.

If we neglect this practice of beginning with silence, our conversation often centers on complaints. Sore muscles, people who have offended, bad drivers, minor disappointments, and such. When we keep silence in the beginning of our run, everything changes. The movement of our bodies becomes a way of praying. One does not have to be still to be meditative, so running in silence teaches us speak to each other with a prayerful respect. We are slow; the trails are rocky and rough. Our speech, contextualized by silence, is gentler than it might have been. In our silent conversations, we become interested in how we provide leadership to the church, how do we refrain from judgment of those who do not share our vision for the community. We recognize the beauty and generosity of our families and friends. Acknowledging our personal struggles, we are even generous with ourselves. Finally, we speak when we have something to say. We do not speak to fill the void.

If silence leads to the love of God, then the love of God must require time. Time, with no agenda, allows affection to rise to the surface of our consciousness. The Bible says that we love God because God loved us first. I don't know how to love God, so for at least twenty-four unbroken hours a week I am available to receive the gift of God loving me.

It is my intent to be welcoming, not demanding—to wait in the silent moment at the construction site, the board meeting, in Nic's living room. I long to learn these things.

I am listening.

At some point during each Sabbath day I become anxious. There is so much to be done. Why am I not doing it? I stop and pick up my prayer beads. I think of Nic. I begin to move them back and forth with my fingers. Prayer begins with silence. I move to the next one, silence leads to the love of God. I am not ready yet. I go back to the beginning, turn the bead over and over, and I wait.

The Jawbone of a Carnivore

Blood spattered my glasses lens and rapidly soaked the front of my pants. I stayed calm. I felt no pain, nothing really. I cut my chainsaw engine and laid it on the ground, then I looked at my right thigh. Even through a couple of now shredded layers of insulated pants, it was easy to see the source of the bleeding. I stretched my fingers into the tear in the pants, poked around the edge of the wound, then ripped the pants open so that I could better assess the damage. I was prepared for anything, I had told Ann. In that state of preparedness, I reached in my back pocket for the only thing I had, a dirty, oil-stained bandana, and used its grimy surface to apply pressure to the bleeding. *This is bad,* I thought. *I wonder how bad. If it's really bad, then I want to start my snow machine and drive it out of the trees and onto the pipeline easement so that if I pass out, someone flying over might see me.*

Small, privately owned, low-flying airplane traffic is common in this part of Alaska's Kenai Peninsula. A floatplane on a lake, tied to a tree in front of someone's house trailer, is not unusual or extraordinary. Believing one of these pilots might see me passed out on the trail—this was what I meant by preparation.

The bleeding slowed, so I unbuckled my pants and pulled them down below my knees. I spread my jacket on the log I had been trimming and sat on it. The nylon was cold on my bare buttocks. I picked up my water bottle and poured the icy, clean water over the wound. A shallow, but wide jagged slice had caused extravagant bleeding; there was blood everywhere. I took the bloody bandana and began to wipe around the edges of the wound. My dog sat calmly and watched, keeping a respectful distance. Frustration and anger combined to make me feel foolish to have made such a dangerous mistake.

I had been clearing a cabin site with my Husqvarna chain saw. A chain saw is held with two hands: one on the handle in the back, and the other grips a metal bar bent over the top. Above the metal bar is a wide, plastic handle. When you hit that handle with the back of your hand, the hand reaching up for the bar, it disengages the chain so it quits turning. The motor is still running but the chain is no longer turning. One of the basic rules of chainsaw use is when you hit it, hit it hard. I didn't. I tapped it with the back of my hand; it slowed but didn't stop. I lowered it to rest on my leg and it ripped a wide stripe of skin off the top of my thigh. A life-threatening moment of carelessness? I didn't know.

Stay calm. There would be a time to think about what I did wrong and what I could do differently, but this was not that time. This was the time to think about what to do next, so I wouldn't make this worse. I skipped ahead to foolish thoughts about helping my wife relax, of how to tell her so that it was not a big deal. This was a helpful, if temporary, means of avoidance. I told myself that on my way home I would stop by the Nikiski Fire Department and have a medic clean my wound so I would not look so dramatic walking into our trailer, as if I could avoid looking dramatic when my pants leg was ripped open and soaked in blood. Next I began to imagine telling Ann this story. She was anxious, with some justification, about the time I spent alone in the outdoors, especially when it involved chain saws. Although Ann would never say, "I told you so," how could she not think it? So much for avoiding the issue.

I stood up, slowed my breathing, reached down and picked up the chain saw, pulled the cord to restart its motor and stepped back onto the log so that I could finish trimming the tree.

My rationale? The bleeding was mostly stopped and I was already out there. Since there would be no avoiding Ann's reaction, I decided that I might as well finish my job. When all the limbs were gone from the tree, I stepped down on the ground and cut the log into easily manageable three-foot sections. This seemed like a good decision. It helped me focus and allowed me to burn the excess energy building up inside from having to acknowledge my own stubbornness. Then I began to gather my gear and put it into the plastic orange kid's sled I pulled behind my snow machine. Chain saw, gas can, axe, sledgehammer, backpack; what else?

I strapped my .45-caliber pistol on my belt. The holster had fallen off when I lowered my pants. I wore it for bear protection. Lotta good it would do if I'd had to run with my pants down.

I managed to remember that I had brought an extra gas can I planned to leave out there.

Our property was nine miles from the nearest road. There were more trees to cut down to clear our cabin site. It would be nice not to have to pack in the extra gas when I came back in the summer. While most folks would travel this trail on a four-wheeler in the summer, we could not afford one, so I would be on foot. I placed the gas can between the exposed roots of a tree, covered it with a plastic tarp, and held it in place with bungee cords.

It was 1982 and I was riding a 1968 Johnson snow machine. It was old but had been reliable. Today, however, it didn't start right away, and it crossed my mind to wonder, with my wound and after the energy expended on the tree, if I was strong enough to walk out. I thought I was, so I was. Finally, the familiar sputter and catch, and the engine took. When it was running smoothly, I looked around to be sure I hadn't forgotten anything, then climbed on, and began the ride to the end of the road, where my truck was parked. The trail was rough and my leg was beginning to hurt, so I was driving slowly with my dog loping behind. I was in an area called Grey Cliffs, nine miles beyond the end of the road and the Captain Cook State Park in Nikiski, Alaska. I had ridden my snow machine on the last weekend that would have adequate snow cover that spring. By next weekend, the long days of sunlight would turn this trail into a muddy bog and it would be much more difficult to navigate.

As I slowly negotiated both the trail and the overall situation, it did occur to me to wonder, *What am I doing out here all alone, clearing a cabin site with a chain saw and no one to help. What if I had cut myself more deeply? I could be dead.* But I knew why I was there and why I was alone. It was a purposeful aloneness. While searching for a new understanding of the love of God in the silence of this extraordinary Alaskan landscape, I was learning that prayer begins with silence, even in a working silence with a chain saw, and although I was not yet articulate about this next step, I was coming to understand that silence leads to the love of God. For much of my life, silence has been a stranger. I talk all the time, far too much with too little thought. So for almost two years I had spent at least one day a week wandering through Grey Cliffs, learning about what God had placed here; tracing creek beds, finding bears, observing moose, wolves, eagles, and owls.

Here, in this particular silence, I pick berries and explore the shores of the many lakes that dot the landscape. This area is bordered by the Cook Inlet, so I wander its shores observing whales, seals, offshore oil platforms, and making friends with the commercial fishermen who spend the summer casting their nets off these beaches, hoping to bring them in full, first of smelt, then herring, and later in the season, salmon.

But it is the silence I am seeking.

It can be hard to get a handle on the love of God. I grew up in an evangelical, Southern, United Methodist environment. As a teenager I made this faith my own. I was well versed in the life of Jesus and believed deeply that his life lived in mine. Loving Jesus was challenging, yet it made sense to me. He stood before me housed in the flesh and blood of humanity. He lived an extraordinary life, and I could hear him calling me to follow him. In my imagination, I can see Jesus calling Zacchaeus down from the tree, comforting the woman at the well, taking the part of the sick and poor as he promises new life to us all. Jesus is a friend who I have come to know and to welcome into the fabric of my daily life. Love for the Creator, God, seems more difficult. How do you measure or even attempt such a thing? Is there any need to? God is too big to measure, as is love. And now, for the first time in my life I am surrounded by folks, many who did not grow up in the church, who are fiercely independent and not at all invested in the orthodoxy in which I was raised. Their broad questioning led me to explore new ways to think and talk about God. They were part of the reason I was wandering Grey Cliffs in a silent quest to calm my mind and encounter the Divine Presence.

When I finally putzed the snow machine back to the trailhead, I lifted myself stiffly off, lowered the tailgate on my pickup truck, backed it up to a snow berm, then drove the snow machine into its bed. As I settled on the seat of the cab, I knew I would follow my somewhat inadequate plan, and stop at the fire department to try and clean up before heading home. I would still enter the house with blood-soaked pants, but at least I could assure Ann the wound was clean.

At that time I was in a phase of life where the things that defined me were sending me and my family on one of the most joyous, adventuresome times we would ever know. The eager tension rising out of the interior of my life was palpable. Longing to follow God, longing for adventure, eager to do what others could not do, I was young, fearless, even brash. Fortunately for us both, my wife, Ann, was also young, fearless, and eager. Fortunately for us both, Ann was often more reasonable and less brash.

I am a United Methodist minister, and on my request I had been appointed to the church that the district superintendent, the bishop's assistant, described as "the smallest church and the worst parsonage in Alaska". Ann and I and our two-year-old son, Chris, loaded our truck, and left Corinth, Mississippi, for Alaska's Kenai Peninsula, where I became the pastor of the North Star United Methodist Church. Prior to this we had never been north of Kentucky. As we prepared to gather a community of people and construct a church building with all local volunteer labor, I decided I needed even more adventure. I joined the Nikiski Fire Department, where I became a firefighter, an emergency trauma technician, and a climber with Nikiski Technical Rescue, all this alongside my primary role as pastor. I wanted more and I wanted less. I wanted more adventure and less noise. I longed to understand what it meant to experience the love of the Creator, God. I believed silence would lead me there, and that I was most likely to become engulfed in silence when I was in motion. So when I read about the Kenai Peninsula Borough Land Disposal program, I knew that was for me.

Less than two percent of the land in Alaska is privately held. Sixty percent is held by the federal government, 25 percent is held by the state and boroughs, and about 13 percent is held by Native corporations. In

1982 the Kenai Peninsula Borough held a land disposal program. The intent was to place more land into private ownership. They designated a block of land called Grey Cliffs and subdivided lots in three different categories: one to three acres, three to ten acres, and ten to forty acres. Residents of the borough were then allowed to purchase up to three tickets that represented particular lots. If your name was drawn in the lottery, you received the right to buy your lot. If you built a structure/cabin that was at least 400 square feet within two years, you received an 80 percent discount on the price of the land. This is as close as a modern-day Alaskan can come to the state's history of homesteading. We wanted to be in on it.

I spent one year in search of silence while walking, simultaneously in search of the perfect lot. Every Friday, my big, yellow, long-haired dog, Cotton, and I would go to Grey Cliffs to explore. We carried the Grey Cliffs Land Disposal map with us as we walked and listened and looked. We rarely saw another person. These days were also my first serious attempt to understand Sabbath keeping. This would be a day unlike other days, intended to renew my spirit. Surely, the silence of this huge, majestic space, the companionship of a good dog, and purposeful wandering would lead me to a new experience of the love of God.

In the winter, we traveled by snow machine even on water frozen into ice. I was astounded to learn about overflow. Often bodies of water, especially moving bodies of water, are not frozen to the bottom. As you cross that frozen river or creek, water is usually flowing deep beneath the ice. When temperatures change or something causes the earth to move, the ice cracks and water comes bubbling up to the top: overflow. The loud noise of a snow-machine engine drowns out the sound of anything as subtle as water running over ice. Sometimes I would cut the engine just to sit and listen. In those lovely moments I could hear birds, the wind blowing in trees, and on the rare occasion, the sound of water, more water, and under ice, more water. It also told me what was safe to cross, and what might not be. This is common knowledge to anyone who lives in the far north but a completely new insight into the way the world works for a twenty-seven-year-old man from Mississippi.

With some surprise, I also learned that bears are not true hibernators. It is not unusual for a bear to get up in the winter, take a hike, search for a snack, and then go back into its den. The first time I saw one walking across a small, open, frozen marsh, I was so excited. I burst into our trailer, my enthusiasm spilling over the kitchen table as I told Ann of this beautiful, surprising sight. My Alaskan friends, who had lived many years in the sub-Arctic, found pleasure in my enthusiastic retelling of things they had long accepted as commonplace. They encouraged me to continue my exploration of the land, and I did. Searching for land where we could build a cabin provided an excuse to wander. Searching for a deeper connection between the physical and the spiritual environment provided a purpose and a reason.

As we explored, Cotton and I found signs of life everywhere and tried to reconstruct the stories from the hints left on the ground. The trail that led to Grey Cliffs was lined with berry bushes: wild blackberries, raspberries, salmon berries with blueberries covering the ground. This trail was a colorful carpet of bear scat. My sense of wonder was heightened by the expectation that the day's explorations would be stalled as I watched bears taking large paws full of berry branches, shoving them into their mouths, then pulling them out, scraping all the berries, leaves, and small branches down their throats. Their mouths were so tough that there was no concern about cuts or scrapes. Despite the brown bears—the much larger coastal cousins of inland grizzlies—and the black bears in this area, the concentration of which was one of the highest in Alaska, there was little fear: with all these berries, moose, and fish, people were too complicated a prey, not worth the trouble when surrounded by rich, easily edible alternatives.

As the end of summer arrived, we had chosen our hoped-for cabin site, and the day of the lottery loomed large in our imagination. That slip of paper would determine who would become Grey Cliffs' landowners. Ann and I were excited by the possibility of this adventure. We had deliberately selected a small patch of land, miles from a road, in an area that was unlikely to be developed in our lifetime. This would be fun, and the modest financial investment would not be a hardship. As I sat in the Kenai High School auditorium, I listened closely, wondering if I knew enough to build a remote cabin, hoping I would get the chance to find out. I watched as the folks in charge reached into a bingo spinner and pulled out a number. Then they reached in another and pulled out a name. There were a lot of names. A lot of numbers.

"Billy Still, lot number 728. Grey Cliffs subdivision."

Leaping up, I dashed forward. Ann had not been able to come. As I held the paperwork and proceeded to finalize the agreement, I was alone and had no one to share my joy, yet we now had the right to purchase 5.8 acres of remote Alaskan property. Ann had often imagined us living far from town in a house on a hill. We now were preparing to purchase this piece of Alaska, a lot that sat on a small bluff on the banks of Otter Creek, where we could create an adventuresome getaway. It was perhaps a half mile from where the mouth of the creek flowed into the Cook Inlet. That creek was filled with trout, and its banks were populated with moose, bears, wolves, berry bushes, and all manner of creation. We could build a cabin as we continued to build our ever-expanding understanding of the deep connection between spirit and land. While this would not exactly be the house of our dreams, it would please us. Besides, our dreams were changing all the time.

Later that summer, after the remaining snow melted and the mud dried up a bit, I loaded my pack, strapped my chain saw to the pack frame, and headed out to make more progress clearing the cabin site. As I approached the tree where I had left the gas can, I noticed that the plastic tarp was gone, yet the gas can remained just as I had left it, snugged tightly between two exposed roots. I slipped my pack off my back and propped it up against another tree, walked over to the gas can and prepared to break it loose from the wet ground and lift it away from the tree. I was startled when a modest tug caused it to fly off the ground, weightless and empty. As I held it up and looked at the bottom, I saw ten clear puncture marks. A bear had lifted it up, punctured the bottom with its claws, and put it right back where it found it. I thought, *Wow, a twenty-mile hike today and I'll get no work done.* My heart smiled. I was not angry or even frustrated; I was just looking for an excuse not to go home this soon. Sitting on a log, I ate a sandwich, relishing the silence and unexpected idleness. I did not want this peace, interrupted only by the sound of water rippling down Otter Creek, to end.

As usual, I was in for a big surprise.

When Cotton and I began the long walk home, we topped a hill where we could see the trail continuing far ahead of us, winding through head-high grass and berry bushes. I looked down at my dog and saw the hair raised on his back, his ears alert, and his tail stiff and still. Once again, he was fulfilling his role as a faithful guide. Cotton lived in a realm I wanted to know. He saw, smelled, and heard things that I didn't. At this moment, he was aware of a threat I recognized only through him. I reached down and clipped the nylon lead to his collar so he wouldn't run off to find it. Scanning the trail in the distance, I noticed a conspicuous-looking black spot a few hundred yards away. Deep mud, I thought, until it stood up and began to walk in my direction. Bears have a great sense of smell and poor vision. The wind was blowing hard our way, so this bear wasn't likely to smell us. I was not going to walk off the trail into the tall grass where I couldn't see, so there was nowhere to go. Common wisdom says it's good to be seen and heard and good to look big, so I began to wave my arms and sing. Having just spent a week at junior high church camp the song that came to mind was: "The Spirit in me greets the spirit in you, Hallelujah. God's in us and we're in God, Hallelujah."

While the singing would let the bear know I was there, the off-key, fearful tremor in my voice would surely scare her off.

Through my brief time in Alaska, I had a variety of ideas about protection from bears.

At first, I carried a shotgun until a friend pointed out that if you were doing anything the shotgun would be leaning against a tree, and unless the bear gave you plenty of notice you would not have time to grab it. If you had time to grab it, you probably didn't need it. Then, for a while I carried a handgun. A .45-caliber bulldog in a holster. The old-timers liked to joke that if you carried a handgun for bear protection, you had five chances to kill the bear. You saved the last bullet for yourself. Realizing that I was not very good with a handgun, imagining a charging bear on the trail and myself face to face with this wounded beast, I quit carrying it, too.

So this was my first day in Grey Cliffs without a gun. All of a sudden, being unarmed doesn't seem like such a good idea. I will have to get lucky. I pray my dog will remain still and quiet. Miraculously, he does.

I find myself recognizing something new about silence…it has a meaning deeper than sound waves bouncing off my eardrums. At this moment my imagination is screaming, "You could be attacked by a bear!" I can hear my heart beating in my chest. The bear, who occasionally woofs for her cubs, seems to be bellowing her displeasure. While none of this is very loud, it creates a disturbance that screams with noisy confusion.

As the bear stepped off the trail into the tall grass, I see that she is followed by three small cubs. The triplets stay on the trail and keep trundling toward Cotton and me. Within ten yards of us, the cubs finally turn and head out into the grass to find their mother. She drops to all fours and I can no longer see her. I decide that I will wait ten minutes and then start walking forward again. I look at my watch. After seven minutes, the sound of blood pounding in my temples tells me that I can wait no longer, there is simply too much tension. Since I cannot stand still, I might as well begin to walk. The world is as silent as I had ever heard it. What happened to the bears? No sight of them, no sound of them, and as my anxiety is resolved, the silence begins to return to my heart.

When it became clear that the bears were gone, I unleashed my dog. Immediately, he charged full speed up the next hill, his hair raised in excitement. Reaching the top of the hill, he threw his front legs to the ground and began uttering a low, guttural growl. Calling him was a waste of time.

He is so fueled by the noisy surge of adrenaline that he is deaf. Unable to see the crest of the hill, I do not know what has elicited such a show of defensive behavior. I assume it is another bear. I sigh. Stay calm, wait. Silence the noise of anxiety. Again, when I run out of patience, I walk up to take a look. Cotton is nose to nose with a large bull moose.

The bull is on its front knees, and they are so close their breath intermingles in the damp air. Each of their heads is frozen, wearing unflinching stares, warrior statues in a wilderness park. This creature carries as much potential danger as the bear. Its rack must be sixty inches across. Bears generally look for a way to avoid a confrontation. Moose act as if the trail is their personal possession. Often they refuse to surrender their space, but in this case, my sudden presence startles the moose, who jumps and runs full speed toward me. I leap off the trail and stumble to the ground. Fortunately, the moose keeps going, whether out of momentum or will I cannot say, but I am grateful for his single-minded claim to his trail. Cotton comes running back to me, licking my face that is still pressed against the soft, cool, muddy ground, and seemingly quite proud of himself for having managed the situation on his terms.

Encounters like this provide a vivid reminder that there is a world beyond the scope of my daily experience. While I am at home paying bills, managing projects, and caring for children, moose and bears roam the landscape, eagles soar, and packs of wolves lay claim to their territory. When returning with friends from jaunts in the outdoors, they often say, "Well, now it's back to the real world," but what if those jaunts into wilderness are the real world? Why is this wild-noised but otherwise silent landscape and the animals that populate it any less real than a day at home?

A breeze moves the tall grass on each side of the trail. The moose and bear disappear into their silent, invisible worlds. Cotton and I share a snack and uneventfully finish our walk to the truck.

The next week, Ann and I head together back to the cabin site. This time with a full gas can, a tent, the chain saw, and a plan to work and explore for several days. On our way out, I tell her the bear story for the umpteenth time. I look down the trail and say, "The bear was right over there, where that bear is." She scolds me for teasing her just as a bear stands, stretches its nose in the air, smells us, and disappears into the grass. While we often think of remote areas as places of silence, we can fail to notice that they are also places of great activity. The movement of plants and animals speak in their own language. Perhaps my task was to learn to hear them.

One day, I observed ravens gathering in the woods just off the trail. I had learned enough to know that they were there for a reason, so we headed over to take a look. It is not unusual for them to feed on an animal kill alongside bears, so we walked slowly and listened carefully. I kept an eye on the dog. Being far more observant than me, he had become my guide. You could tell when he was excited or uncomfortable. The hair on the back of his neck would stand at attention, his ears rise up in an alert position, his tail became stiff and still, all of the physical signs pointing to 'ready', his form of warning and preparation. He seemed relaxed and happy today. His body told mine that it was okay to breathe easy.

As we stepped into a clearing, the ravens took off and I saw an old moose kill. Bones were scattered about, and only small patches of the tough moose hide remained. It was clear that a wide variety of animals had been feeding on this carcass for some time. These modest remnants would be beyond the interest of a bear. We relaxed and began to explore, me doing my best to reconstruct the skeleton laying on the ground. As I gathered and identified bones, I came upon a surprising find: the jawbone of a carnivore.

Wolf, coyote, or feral dog, I wasn't sure. But it was one of those. I sat on a log turning this jawbone over in my hands, and in my imagination I began to reconstruct the scene that caused this canine to die on a moose kill. Perhaps a pack of wolves was attacking the moose, and this unlucky predator received a fatal kick to the head. Maybe this beast was feeding on the moose kill when a bear returned to claim its prize and—finding a competitor—killed and ate it, too. Could it be that an unlucky coyote was nibbling on the edges of a freshly killed feast when the wolf pack returned?

I didn't know, but as I sat on the log I found myself overwhelmed with love. A web of life and death exists, often invisibly, all around me. How had I lived so long and seen so little? I looked again and found signs of mice nibbling on bones and ants, bugs, worms, who knows what had lived and died on the back of this once magnificent creature? What I came to know is that much of creation spins on its axis each day without regard for me or you. I felt myself reoriented from the small-minded thinking that places me at the center of the universe. While my love of Jesus reminds me that God is compassionately concerned for the detail of my daily life, this encounter with life and death reminded me that I am a minuscule dot in the broader circle of creation. When I stopped to listen to the wind, the small sounds in the grasses, the earth itself, I heard also this moose, singing songs of the vital energy of creation, even in death.

As I turned the jawbone over in my hands, and looked out over the site, I found the moose's lower jaw. I reached, then stopped. I decided to leave it as it lay. There were flowers growing between the teeth and ants were polishing the hinge of the jaw. Already, in the short time the moose had been dead, it was providing the nourishment for new life. The prophet Isaiah spoke the word of God saying, "I am about to do a new thing. It is springing forth from the bud. Can you not perceive it?"

I was learning to perceive it.

Is it helpful to say that silence leads to the love of God? It's helpful for me. For several years I wandered through Grey Cliffs for days at a time. Sometimes with Ann, always with Cotton, and rarely with the rattle of words. I came to see the world in a radically different way. I began to understand that my emotionally driven orientation toward movement and adventure could become great life assets. They were gifts offered to me from the hands of a generous Creator. I was energized when exploring new places. I did not miss the sound of people's voices. When far off the road, even days away from other people, I was comfortable, relaxed and hyperaware of my surroundings. There was much to be learned, and I was and remain primed to learn it. In the presence of this active silence I sensed the presence of an active love.

The untraveled world pulls relentlessly at my heart as it unplugs the ears of my soul. A silent observation of life allows me to hear and fall in love with the voice of a world previously unknown. So I thought, and think, prayer begins with silence and silence leads to the love of God, the thoughtful creator of all that is.

For a number of years there was a light scar across the top of my right thigh. A sign of what happens when I become careless and unfocused. Over decades of healing, old skin peels off, new skin takes its place thousands of times across the years, and the scar is now too faint to be seen. But I do not want to forget that the healing silence brings is a place to begin; it is no place to stop. Surely the love of God leads us to something new. A new way to understand ourselves and a new way to live in relationship with creation and the people who populate it. Could it be that the love of God leads to the love of our neighbor? If that is true, then where must I wander next?

I Can Choose Peace

Doodling, looking out the window, making up stories, throwing paper wads at other kids, being completely disengaged from the teacher's agenda for the classroom—that was school. As our geometry teacher stood in the front of the class, writing formulas on the board, my wandering eyes explored the landscape beyond the borders of the classroom. I tapped increasingly complex Steve Gadd-worthy rhythms with my pencil on the desk. I drew pictures on random pages. I watched sparrows sparring in the trees. I wondered who drove the cars that passed those windows. Where did they get the freedom to drive around in the middle of the day? I watched anything that moved. Eventually, I would look at the board and anxiously realize that I had no idea what she was talking about.

I feel a familiar sense of alarm. In the past thirty minutes, I haven't heard a word she has spoken and I am lost. I can't ask a question because I don't know what the topic is. My whole body screams, "Don't make eye contact!" A silence reigns in the classroom, and my resolve crumbles. I look up and see her staring at me. Our eyes meet. She points at me and orders me to stay and speak with her after class. Later, as I stand nervously beside her desk, she tells me that she will do whatever it takes to help me pass her class. In response, I am to agree not to take any more math classes.

"Billy, you just can't do math," she says.

At some place, in the core of my spirit, as shame and anger boil over, I decide that she is right, I can't do math. I begin to wonder, *What else is there that I cannot do?*

Slamming the door of the portable classroom, I storm out recklessly, riding a wave of adolescent rage. I do not care what my teacher thinks as she watches through the window and I throw my notebook against the outside wall. Papers fly across the school lawn like dead leaves blowing in that October Jackson, Mississippi, wind. Not bothering to pick them up, I march defiantly down the sidewalk, climb into my car and abandon the school campus. Having nowhere to go I just drive, too angry, too fast, not caring that a car is a dangerous place to express frustration and rage, not caring that I will surely get into trouble for skipping an afternoon of school. Perhaps I won't ever come back. Why bother?

My experience in that geometry class became a caricature of my experience in all the classrooms of life. While I continued to be physically present at school and even made acceptable grades, on that fall afternoon in 1969, standing on the sidewalk of Wingfield High School with a turbulent sense of powerlessness and no sense of purpose, I quit. From then on I would get by and that would be enough.

This frustration and defiance was not new. I had spent much of my short life developing the anger that exploded that day. On occasion, I still feel its rumblings. It first became apparent to me as I joined my parents in attending parent teacher conferences at Sykes Elementary School. A deep, passionate dread rose in my childish spirit as we drove to school to sit and listen to a set of consistent and thoroughly frustrating observations. Teachers spoke to my parents about me as if I were not present.

71

"Mr. and Mrs. Still, it's not that he is not smart enough to do the work. I think that he is very smart. If he would just sit down, be still, be quiet, pay attention, and turn in his work on time, everything would be fine."

Those words stung each time I heard them and I heard them often. I heard them from teachers, coaches, Sunday School teachers, and my parents. My father suggested that the modesty of our success as hunters and fishermen hinged on my inability to remain focused, still, and quiet. "Billy be quiet, Billy be still, Billy pay attention, Billy quit playing around and do your work," became accusatory mantras the adult world flung in my direction. When I would listen to them, I would hang my head while my imagination screamed, *I have no idea how to do these things! Somebody, please quit telling me what to do and show me how to do it!*

From the eyes of an adult I can see that my parent-teacher conferences were frustrating for my parents too. "Why won't you simply do as you are told?" they wondered out loud, mistaking my frustration for resistance.

My teachers were committed to doing their job with the least classroom disruption possible. Everyone sat in straight rows while the teacher wrote on the chalkboard. Don't fidget, move, talk, or let your mind wander. Just look straight ahead and pay attention. My inadequate response came to a head on the day a geometry teacher, whose name I have mercifully forgotten, said to me with unquestioned authority, "Billy, you just can't do math." She was the teacher; I believed her; I quit doing math.

When my wife, Ann, and I began to join our children for their parent-teacher conferences, I was committed to creating an experience different than mine. This was not a simple task. When I walked into my children's classroom, I could hear a patronizing voice from the past saying, "Billy, you just can't do math."

In the 1950s and 1960s in public schools in Mississippi, no one spoke of Attention Deficit Hyperactivity Disorder. Although I have never been formally diagnosed, when people began using this language to describe the behavior of our oldest son, Chris, I knew exactly what they were talking about. When we went to his first, second-grade, parent-teacher conference, I carried my childish anxiety into the room like a flag. My emotional antennas were flying high, and it did not take much for his teacher to set off the alarms.

"Mr. and Mrs. Still, it's not that Chris is not smart enough to do the work. I think that he is very smart. If he would just sit down, be still, be quiet, pay attention, and turn his work in on time, everything would be fine."

I gulped deeply as I tried to untie the knot forming in my stomach. How did I reconcile the tension in my tightening throat with the calm voice I so wanted to project? Ann, familiar with this struggle in my life, recognized the tension before I spoke and began to pat my leg under the table, knowing that physical contact would help me stay calm. Chris was not going to spend the next ten years listening to this! I suggested that it would be helpful if we could teach him how to do those things instead of criticizing him for not doing them. To her credit she agreed, spoke beyond the tension in my voice, and referred us to a pediatrician. This pediatrician saw many children from Tudor Elementary School, and Chris's teacher was confident that she could help. We called the next day for an appointment and were able to see her the next week.

On the day we saw the doctor, Chris was quite tense. So was I. I'm sure that Ann, wife and mother, the gentle voice in our family, was tense, too. She was hoping that I would relax and be calm. We were all hoping to identify a practical path to Chris's academic and behavioral success. I am confident now that I was trying to quell some of the ghosts of my past. There was a sense of guilt that I carried. He's having a hard time in school just like I did. It must be my fault. The doctor walked in, said hello, read the teacher's referral papers, and said, "Mr. and Mrs. Still, I am going to write Chris a prescription for Ritalin. This will help him focus and control his behavior. He will do better in school. Let's make a follow-up appointment to monitor his dosage."

"How long will he need to take this?" I asked.

"Probably until he is an adult," she casually replied.

Not a chance. This is a little boy. Her recommendation was far too casual.

During my senior year at Wingfield High School, many things began to change for me. For the first time in my life I embraced the Christian faith as my own. There was a developing drive to become a follower of Jesus Christ that existed independent of my parents or our local church. Along with that drive, I received an internal confidence that I would become a pastor in the United Methodist Church, the denomination in which I had been raised. The phrase, common in our religious tradition, called by God, carried with it a deep sense of purpose. This calling became the driving force that directed my growing desire to embrace the why of my life. As this grew, my interest in school changed. It dawned on me that an ordained UMC pastor must graduate from seminary, and therefore I must go to college. I applied to Millsaps College with this single-minded ambition: I must be a pastor, I must go to seminary to become a pastor, and I must graduate from college before I can go to seminary. My ACT and SAT scores were high enough to compensate for my modest high school grades. Through the years this ability to test well had enabled me to climb many hurdles. My acceptance to Millsaps College was the next stake driven into the pathway that marked the route to my vocational goal. It was a stake driven in with a series of wavering blows. While I could envision the end result—me, an ordained pastor—I could not envision being able to negotiate the path that would take me there.

While I was a student at Millsaps, I began to care about academic learning with a newly acquired desire. During registration the first semester of my freshman year, I was given a copy of Ernst Cassirer's *An Essay on Man* and instructed to read it prior to our first class, three days away. These were the days when college registration involved standing in line in the gym for hours at a time. Cassirer develops a theory of symbolism in his book and uses it to expand phenomenology of knowledge into a more general philosophy of culture. As I read these words in the prologue, my heart struggled between the thrill of possibility and the fear of failure. I wondered, *Can I do this, or is it like math?* I longed to know what Cassirer was saying and why it was important. I read An Essay on Man in most waking moments until I was able to summarize his arguments in my head. While I have long lost the subtlety of his logic, that weekend I came to believe that I could learn at a high level. Perhaps I could do math.

The first semester my sophomore year I was confronted with science requirements for BA students, and in the struggle to find a place where I might succeed I registered for an astronomy class. Millsaps College is in downtown Jackson, Mississippi, my hometown. It has an observatory on campus, and each time our family went downtown I had looked at the observatory and longed to go inside. Without giving it too much thought, I imagined sitting in the seat and rotating the giant telescope as I waved at the man on the moon. By this time I wanted to look through the telescope at the stars. There was only one way to do that: one must take astronomy at Millsaps, so I did. On the first day of class, we reviewed the course syllabus. The next day we toured the observatory. It was just as I had imagined it: a large elevated seat facing a huge telescope. It had been built so long ago that it still had a hand crank that you turned to move the lens from side to side. The next day, we began to learn how one can identify a planet or star and then arrange the telescope so that it will find it at a particular time of day. This required math. When the instructor told us that we would need to interpolate, my mind went blank. I can't do math! I saw my high school geometry teacher standing in front of me, leaning against her desk, and could hear her say, "Billy what are you doing here? You promised no more math classes. You know you can't do math!" In fear and frustration, I went to a friend in the dormitory and asked for help.

"Phillip," I asked, "What does it mean to interpolate?"

He replied somewhat like this, "Interpolation is a method of constructing new data points within the range of a discrete set of known data points."

After some reflection and several brief, anxious conversations, to my overwhelming surprise I found that I understood what he was saying. He showed me how the formula worked, and I discovered that I could do it. I could do math! Who knew? Certainly not me, not my geometry teacher. Phillip did not know that I couldn't. What I did not understand was why this was so difficult for me. It did not seem to be challenging at all for Phillip. He was smart, but I thought I was just as smart. Yet what could have been obvious years before was just becoming clear to me, I don't learn like other people. I thought that meant that there was something wrong with me, after all, it was somebody's fault...wasn't it?

Years later, as we sat in the doctor's office with our son, Chris, in the next room, Ann and I looked at each other with alarm. I asked the doctor if she did not want to do some testing, talk to Chris, get to know him before taking such a step. She assured us that she knew what she was doing and that this was the right answer. While Ann and I were not opposed to using prescription medication as a last resort, we knew we would never agree to this as a first response. On the way out of her office I threw the prescription in the trash. In my imagination I could see the papers from my math notebook flying across the lawn of Wingfield High School. However, this was different. I determined that Chris did not have to go through school feeling guilty about the way he did, or did not, do his work. He was not required to believe something was wrong with him. I could not give up on Chris. Ann and I knew we must find the skills to shepherd him through this process.

When we returned home, we made an appointment with a child psychologist who was recommended by our family pediatrician, and who assured us that she would spend time with Chris, engage him in a series of evaluative tests, and then we would decide together which responses would be most helpful.

We went to her office with a commitment to be hopeful, yet I struggled to set aside my childhood trauma and to embrace the possibilities that waited for Chris in school. I was not sure I could do this until Ann reminded me that this decision was about Chris, not me. Perhaps, but did she know Chris and I shared a secret? Ann was an excellent student who graduated from Millsaps magna cum laude in three years. What did she know about struggling to learn?

After a family interview and then some time alone with Chris, the psychologist took him to a room for testing. In my mind's eye, I could see Chris looking at the papers, fidgeting, doodling in the margins, tapping his pencil, then looking up, refocusing, and doing a bit more. How would he fare?

When we returned for the next visit she shared with us that the tests revealed Chris was mildly ADHD. Although I had heard that phrase before, it was not as common in the early 1980s as it is now. This was the first time I heard anyone speak of it with any specificity. Even as I wondered what this meant for Chris, I simultaneously included my own awareness that I didn't learn like others. Applying this knowledge to our son became the first time I used it to come to a deeper understanding of myself!

The psychologist was calm and relaxed. She put down her clipboard and encouraged us to receive this as good news. It meant we could identify a particular learning style that was Chris's and then button down specific learning techniques that would help him be successful in school. She was positive, and never once spoke of what he could not do. I felt the tension drain from my body; the knot in my stomach loosened when it became clear that she was not going to say, "Mr. and Mrs. Still, it's not that he is not smart enough to do the work. I think that he is very smart. If he would just sit down, be still, be quiet, pay attention, and turn in his work on time, everything would be fine."

The psychologist provided us with a list of things that would help Chris focus on his work. She believed and we agreed that mastering these skills would serve him better than altering his behavior with drugs. We left with a confidence that Chris could learn behavioral and environmental adaptations that would help him cope. For now, we would not use drugs to calm him down and risk dulling his vigorous imagination. Things we could do included engaging his teacher in identifying ways his classroom experience could be redesigned. Things as simple as the placement of his desk would help. I left with the secret hope that I could learn some additional coping mechanisms that would ease the strain of my work and my relationship with Ann and the kids.

As a Millsaps student whose primary purpose was to earn a bachelor's degree so that I could go to the seminary, I was on shaky ground. At the end of my sophomore year I received a humorous award from some of my friends. They said I had a perfect grade point average: 4.0 each of my first two years. That's two points each semester. I knew that a solid C would not be good enough to gain entrance to graduate school. The thrill of intellectual challenge that I received from Ernst Cassirer had not translated into helpful study skills. I knew that I must learn to study, and the time was now. It was hard work to silence the familiar voices that said, "Mr. and Mrs. Still, it's not that he is not smart enough to do the work. I think that he is very smart. If he would just sit down, be still, be quiet, pay attention, and turn in his work on time, everything would be fine."

I wanted desperately to do these things; however, I had not made much progress in recognizing the clues that would lead me to success. Over the next few months, I began to take notes about what happened when I became distracted. Sitting at my desk I would look up, realize I was lost, then write a sentence or two about my experience. While in class I would make a note about when I was engaged and when I was not. Sometimes, I would decide to remove distractions from my desk or walk to refocus and write down if that was helpful or not. On those moments when I felt fulfilled and successful, I would do my best to clarify why and how these moments were different from others. I realized that the satisfaction of completing the simplest task lifted my self-esteem. Working from those observations, I created a list of corrective responses. While I do not have a copy of my original list, or of Chris's, they both look somewhat like this:

1. Remove visual distractions.
2. Remove auditory distractions.
3. Create deadlines for myself.
4. Create a list of interim goals.
5. While working on big projects, keep a list of small, easily accomplished tasks close at hand.
6. When I get stuck, stand up, clean my work area, walk around the block, and come back right away.

With these things in mind, my study times began to look different. I would sit at a clean desk facing a wall, not a window. I would often play music to block out background noise, being careful that it did not have words to distract. I created deadlines that were significantly earlier than the required deadlines. This helped me avoid some crises and provided time to cope with the ones that inevitably arose. There was a notepad on my desk that listed four or five simple, short tasks. When I needed a break I would check them off, creating a sense of accomplishment. When I got stuck and could not move forward, I cleaned and walked. While this did not always lead to academic success, it provided a platform for a significant leap forward. My last two years, my grade-point average vastly improved.

Chris's list was so similar to mine that it was uncanny. As I read it over and over, I felt a new depth of empathy for this little boy who wouldn't turn in his homework. I also experienced the beginning of real empathy for the Wingfield High School student who couldn't do math, as well as for the Millsaps student who waded through all of this alone, determined to fulfill his calling to ministry.

Throughout life, as I reach for my particular stride on the pathway to peace, I am likely to find that there are some stumbling blocks that are mine to keep. I have learned that, like the color of my eyes, learning is not a fleeting issue. There will never be a time that I am not required to pay attention to the difference between the way most folks present information and the way I process it. These are lessons that I learned slowly over time, and that I learn to reframe at every stage of life. As I have matured, I have acquired various coping mechanisms that compensate for the liabilities of my learning style. I have also identified ways that being wired for my own way of learning is an asset, not a liability. This awareness broadened my understanding far beyond academic exercises. I realized that my learning style had a significant impact on relationships, even our marriage. It was not just a pedantic matter; it was an amazing discovery.

For example, early in our marriage I would come home and without comment begin to straighten the house. Ann did not appreciate my cleaning, and I did not understand why. This reached a crisis point during the time we lived in Anchorage, Alaska. It was no small task to maintain an orderly home with three children in the winter in Alaska. Without realizing it, I was simply trying to create a space, a nest, a clean, clear zone around a chair where I could sit for a few minutes and relax, my environment and therefore my mind uncluttered. Ann interpreted this behavior as criticism of the way that she, a stay-at-home mom, cared for the house. I'm confident that there were times I sent this message as I stacked newspapers and magazines with unnecessary force. As odd as it now seems, it took several years for Ann and me to find a way for each of us to take responsibility for ourselves and not to offer or take offense.

All of us have issues that are part of the definition of who we are, and therefore they remain with us forever. I will always have to work hard to concentrate as I do math. There will never be a time when it is not important for me to do major projects in an orderly environment. There have been countless days like the one spent waiting for Nic to arrive, struggling to balance my impatience in a healthy relational way with others and our conflicting priorities. Wandering across the land in Grey Cliffs or wherever we lived at the time heals broken places in my heart and mind. This purposeful movement calms my spirit, even as it reflects my anxiety. I continue to be moved as I remember that on the eve of what would become their greatest crisis, Jesus spoke to his followers and said, "Peace I leave with you; my peace I give to you. I do not give to you as the world gives. Do not let your hearts be troubled, and do not let them be afraid."

When I hear this, my disorganized heart responds with the cry of my continuing struggle, "Where did you leave this peace? I can't seem to find it! I can't do math and I can't be still!"

How beautiful it has been to abandon the myth with which I have lived much of my life. The myth that for me to experience peace I must resolve all the issues that I find troubling. This led me to believe that things like my learning style must change. To be well and live in peace, I must begin to learn like others. It has been a tremendous relief to abandon that way of thinking. At this stage in life, I have come to see my particular learning style as a gift—a sometimes complicated and unwelcome gift, but a gift nonetheless. It provides me with great surges of energy, curiosity, and creativity. It becomes a lifeboat as long as I keep its flood of emotional possibility within the banks of my life's river. What I cannot do is live with the expectation or even desire that it will go away. So I stand up and name the challenging things in my life that risk robbing me of peace and that will never go away. When I name them and the disruptive possibilities that follow them, I can receive the counsel of Dr. Wayne Dyer, look at these disruptive forces, and say, "I can choose peace rather than this."

For fifteen years I was the senior pastor of St. Paul's United Methodist Church in Tucson, Arizona. I was the big-picture guy and was fortunate to have a marvelous staff that cared for the details. For fourteen of those years, Angie McCarty was the primary associate pastor. Early in my ministry I had made a decision that when I wanted to talk to someone on the church staff, I would go to their office instead of asking them to come to mine. I had once served on a church staff where the senior pastor would have the secretary call me and summon me to his office. Without being invited to sit, I would be given the necessary information and then would be dismissed with a curt, "That is all." I do not know what he thought of me or my work. I was young, and I was trying to prove myself and while I received significant affirmation from others, I longed for one good word from him. It stung when it was withheld. I wanted a different kind of relationship with our staff. This was easy with Angie. We worked together seamlessly, often working for hours at a time on projects. We didn't just design worship, we designed worship series, classes, and strategies for exploring the life of the church, often planning the flow of worship and classes up to eighteen months in advance. She was a stickler for detail, which made us well-suited partners in these tasks.

When we first began this work, I would go to her office. After all, this is the principle I had decided on. It would be a way to shift the balance of power in her direction and smooth out the distance in our age and levels of experience. She was extremely bright and eager, and I didn't want to do anything that might dampen her vigorous enthusiasm.

I would walk into her office, but then I didn't know what to do. Chairs were full of papers and books. Unopened packages were stacked indiscriminately on the floor. Leftover documents from previous programs were stacked in corners. Simply put, I didn't know where to sit or stand. In a state of carefully disguised fluster, I would return to my office or take a walk around the campus. How could I work to level the playing field of office, experience, job title, and power, and at the same time affirm her extraordinary leadership skills? It would be out of line for me to request that she keep her office like mine, because her style worked well for her. At the same time, I knew I could not do my best work in that environment.

One morning I went in to address this issue. I was stumbling around, trying not to offend…with several false starts.

Finally, she laughed, "Just tell me what you want to discuss." She poked fun at me when I described the issue, and as was our pattern, asked what we could do to make it better.

We began to work in my office. I placed a chair beside my desk that we thought of as hers. It symbolized the balance of power we were searching for and at the same time allowed me to control the space surrounding us. I could clean my desk and the shelves around this work area, having nothing there but the project at hand. Most importantly, I could do this without criticizing Angie as I took responsibility for myself. This may seem like a small issue; however, if you are one of those folks who fear all the papers in the pile behind you may take on a life of their own as they rise up and subvert your current project, it's really important.

I am in my mid-sixties and still pay attention to these issues daily. I work from home, and my desk is clean and orderly; most days I straighten it before I leave. I have learned to manage these things. They are part of who I am, and if I neglect them, I subvert my ability to live in peace.

Often, when I struggle with a task and a deadline, I stop and pray. I hear Jesus offering peace and assuring me that I can learn to experience this peace. "Peace I leave with you; my peace I give to you. I do not give to you as the world gives. Do not let your hearts be troubled, and do not let them be afraid." These familiar words come back to me and I am surprised to hear, once again, that I can choose not to let my heart be troubled. I can choose not to be afraid. I can choose peace.

When the voices ghost my mind, Mr. and Mrs. Still, it's not that he is not smart enough to do the work. I think that he is very smart. If he would just sit down, be still, be quiet, pay attention, and turn in his work on time, everything would be fine. Or when I hear the voices saying, Billy, you just can't do math, I get up from my desk, clean my work area, then take a quick walk around the block. I take a look at my short and easy task list. I select two tasks, accomplish them, check them off the list, and then turn back to the primary task at hand.

There are other voices to silence. Some far more difficult than this one. When I face them I remember: I can do math, and I can choose peace rather than this.

Smudges on the Windshield

As pastors of St. Paul's United Methodist Church in Tucson, Arizona, Angie and I stood side by side on Sunday morning for fourteen years. An easy banter flowed between us. We held such a deeply shared understanding of leadership and friendship that there were days we even preached together. Above all else, we declared hope. We declared hope as I struggled with heart disease and the various interventions and surgical procedures required to keep me alive. We declared hope as her life was occasionally covered in the long veil of depression. Along with the author of the Gospel of John, we boldly proclaimed that the light shines in the darkness and the darkness does not overcome it. We told the truth about these matters, knowing that the room was full of people with similar struggles. The love of God called us to announce that all of these things are best realized through the covenant of a community, committed to each other. While we know to hold onto hope as tightly as one can, the covenant is sometimes broken and hope is hard to find. In those times, hope rests on a long arch that stretches across the narrative that is life.

While we served our pastoral roles, alongside us our spouses found their places of service. They were faithful members of the congregation, announcing hope in their own way as leaders in the church. Oftentimes her husband would play guitar in the band. While he was playing and Angie and I were leading worship; Ann, often with the assistance of our two younger children, adolescents at the time, would care for their three

87

children, ushering them back and forth to worship, nursery, and Sunday School.

On this particular Sunday, Angie stood before the new congregation where she had been the senior pastor for just one year. I was recently retired and her volunteer pastoral helper.

Reading from Psalm 137, she joined the people of ancient Israel, captives taken into exile, and she wailed along with them, embracing broken hearts:

"By the rivers of Babylon – there we sat down and there we wept when we remembered Zion… How could we sing the Lord's song in a foreign land?"

Then she said, "Today, I must tell you that my husband of fifteen years is leaving our marriage. He has told me that he is going to move out and file for divorce." As collective sadness fell over the congregation, it felt as if a dark fog rolled in from the back. She spoke of the desire for grace, requesting that we respond to him with kindness and her children with tolerance and support as they braved a crisis over which they had no control. When her emotions overwhelmed her, and she could speak no longer, she invited me to come and lead the community in prayer. Then she took her seat on the front row. Like the people of ancient Israel, the tears silently ran down her cheeks, overflowing the banks of a river that was dark and unknown. At this moment she longed to be somewhere else, but knowing she was required to wait and receive the compassion of this congregation she tended, she could not help but wonder, how could she sing the Lord's song in this foreign land?

And my own question: how would I help her do that? Although I did not know where it would lead, I did know that God's plan for our immediate futures was far from the plans we had crafted. Angie, Ann, the kids, and I were going learn to lean heavily on each other for comfort and support.

As I did my best to stand beside her and enter into her pain, I had no idea what lay ahead.

She must embrace the challenge of creating a new life for herself while parenting her children, who would be with her only half the time. She would also struggle to meet the expectation that she bravely cry out the promise of hope to a church full of people, many of whom were anxious about their own marriages, while they wondered what happened to their pastor's. Before me would come the opportunity to follow the biblical admonition to be provoked to good works, as I tried to find a way to let the love of God lead me somewhere that mattered. I did not know I would be led to a new adventure in loving my neighbor, caring for my pastor, my friend, and her children. I too did not know where in this foreign land, I would be led. Newly retired, this was not what I expected in retirement.

Today was one of the simple days. Angie wanted to take her kids on a campout, and my car was a better camping car. We had switched cars, and I got mine back on Saturday afternoon. When I climbed into the driver's seat, I looked up and noticed that there were smudges on the windshield. Not little smudges but thick distracting ones that made it difficult to see as the sun shone bright on this Sonoran Desert winter afternoon in Tucson, Arizona. I reached under the front seat where I kept an old towel and grabbed it to try to wipe them off. I wiped over and over before I realized that they were on the outside of the windshield. What were they? As I sat back and looked, I began to see them more clearly. Five toes, the ball of the foot, and imprints of a little heel. Brendan. Had he been walking on the windshield? Oh my.

Brendan is six years old. He has a nine-year-old brother, Jackson, and a twelve-year-old sister, Addison. My wife, Ann, was present, holding their mother's hand at each of their births. Ann and I were their first babysitters. Their births sealed the friendship that existed between our families. Although we were already close, after the births we began to spend holidays together and vacation with each other. We also kept their children when they wanted time away. They have been strong supporters to Ann and me as I have endeavored to live through my adventures with heart disease with dignity. We have joined them as they have done their best to embrace two careers, three young children, and vastly different expectations of how life is to be lived. Angie remains one of our closest friends.

After filing for divorce, the kids' dad chose to live in a rental house a few blocks away. The first day the kids are to spend the night at Dad's new house is also the day of Brendan's family birthday party. Each child has two birthday parties: one with their friends, and one with the important adults in their lives. This second one is known as the family birthday party. There was a certain amount of tension surrounding the question of Dad's presence. Would he come or not? When Ann and I arrived, we did not know. It was a question each guest pondered.

He didn't come. Brendan cried.

While I boil with internal anger toward him, I also try to consider his dilemma more carefully, and slowly a twinge of compassion rises. If I were him, I would not want to come to a dining room full of bright balloons and candles and cake, people who I felt did not understand me and who had little interest in trying. Everyone here would be friendly and kind. Perhaps too much so. As we pass pieces of birthday cake, his absence is as vivid as his presence would have been. But we do not express this. We all realize that it is important to accept a certain careful compartmentalization of feelings and behavior. He is the kids' dad. When I am with him, I am courteous and kind. This courtesy has nothing to do with how I feel. Determined to do the right thing, I'm often not sure what that means. This foreign land is new ground for me.

As the party winds down, Angie receives a text. Dad is outside at the end of the driveway. Will she send the kids out for their time with him? She shows me the text, wondering what to do. Just send them out or insist he come in to get them? I have no idea what is best. What will be appropriate a year from now might not be required today. Feelings are fresh; wounds still bleed. She decides to make it easy on everyone and send them out.

Jackson, the middle child, will have none of this. "This is my house!" he announces. "I will not leave." Angie finds herself in the peculiar position of negotiating on Dad's behalf; convincing Jackson to do that thing she hates the most: leave their home with their dad, for a week, for the first time. It will not be the last. Finally, Jackson goes, carrying his wounds as well as those of his brother and sister like a flag. A river of tears washes away all of the familiar signs of family life. We are all wandering through this foreign land.

But in time a pattern develops. Transitions take place each Friday afternoon at 5:30.

Angie and Dad work this out, always displaying the appearance of peace while the emotional disruption it creates is like roadkill carelessly strewn across the highway exit ramp that is their life.

For the most part, the inevitable struggles and arguments that rise out of their divorce take place in private. While the children certainly recognize rising tension, they do not hear one parent speak poorly about the other. Both mom and dad are committed to their children never having to choose which one to love. Still, it is confusing for little minds to sort out the meaning behind this kind of separation. It is confusing for adult minds, too.

A few days later, Brendan asks his mom, "Why doesn't Daddy love us anymore?" He refuses to look up or make eye contact.

His mom replies, "Oh, honey. Your daddy loves you."

"Then why doesn't he live here anymore?"

"You will need to ask him. He will tell you why."

This bewildering answer provided no satisfaction for anyone. It didn't help Brendan or the other kids, who clumsily pretended they were not paying attention while listening intently. I flinched internally as I listened, and I knew Angie well enough to know that her gut was tightening, too. The various commitments she and their dad had made roared into conflict. Angie was committed to telling the truth; the divorce was not mutually agreed upon. Both parents were committed to never speaking poorly of the other one in front of the children or in public with friends. These various commitments created an uneasy tension. There were parts of the story that were not hers to tell. Dad would have to explain why he left.

Brokenness lurks around every corner; you must be careful where you step. With divorce comes the inevitable question, "Who gets the friends?" I know the ideal is that everyone will remain friends with them both. That idealistic notion is rarely revealed in practice. None of us knows how this works until we begin to figure out who calls back. Ann and I are so closely associated with Angie and the kids that this affects us, too. A few guys I used to run or ride bikes with are no longer available on the days I can go. This makes me sad but not angry. It carries with it a minor sense of relief. We get to avoid talking about this by keeping distance. Not unlike Dad, acting out a self-imposed exile while avoiding eye contact, kicking rocks around at the end of the driveway.

I have spoken of a particular cycle of praying: Prayer begins with silence, silence leads to the love of God, and the love of God leads to the love of our neighbor. How does loving God lead to loving my neighbor in this situation? It's easy to see how the love of God leads to new ways of loving between me, Angie, Ann, and the kids. But how am I to be a neighbor to the ones who won't call back? Perhaps they are thinking the same thing about me. Billy won't call back since Angie's divorce.

If this spiritual progression makes sense, then the peace that Jesus offers must exist smack dab in the middle of life as it is, not life as I wish it were. There is no room for avoidance. This doesn't mean that life cannot, should not, or will not change. It means Jesus's peace is not dependent upon how I would like life to be.

"I do not give it as the world gives," he said on the eve of his execution.

Tension exists in our households, and tension lives between the vast, mysterious creator of all that is and the God with intimate knowledge, concern, and compassion for each of us. A love for God that invites us to embrace both of these truths leads us to love our neighbor.

So how to implement that? Love Angie and the kids. That's easy. They call, we hang out, we give rides and provide the presence of other needed adults. Often it is a quite practical expression of love. Love Dad? We have little contact except for child exchanges. It's civil. Is that love? Love the friends who won't call back or the ones with whom I now avoid contact... keep a distance that either protects or negates or allows for healing.

I am not sure which is most real, and that's harder. I desperately want to live in this tension with integrity.

In the tenth chapter of the Gospel of Luke, Jesus is confronted by an expert in religious law. The Israel of Jesus's day was an occupied territory. The Roman occupation was long, and there was no end in sight. The religious officials of Israel had negotiated a civil peace agreement that recognized Roman law and their religious law. Our cherished separation of church and state would have seemed odd to them. It was in this context that a religious lawyer approached Jesus with a question.

"Teacher, what must I do to inherit eternal life?"

"What does the law say?" Jesus replied.

"You shall love the Lord your God with all your heart, and all your soul, and all your strength, and all your mind, and you shall love your neighbor as yourself," Jesus affirmed his answer and encouraged him to live this way.

Then the lawyer asked, "But who is my neighbor?"

Jesus's response became one of his most well known parables: the parable of the Good Samaritan. It is a story of complex interactions embedded in a simple truth: the true neighbor is the one who helps. A man is mugged, and all the traditional heroes walk on by. Imagine a police officer and your local pastor acting as if you are not there. And you are too wounded to speak. Then comes the traditional enemy, a Samaritan. Jews and Samaritans had historic contempt for each other. In Jesus's telling, the Samaritan stops to help the man in trouble. This Samaritan goes far beyond any reasonable expectation of compassion as he helps the man in need. When Jesus makes the Samaritan the hero of the story, everyone is ill at ease.

"Which of these was a neighbor to the man who fell into the hands of robbers?"

They couldn't quite bring themselves to say 'the Samaritan' so they answered, "The one who showed him mercy."

Loving God with all my heart, soul, mind, and strength has little meaning if it does not lead to loving my neighbor as myself. Beyond that, the parable has dual meaning. We are also invited to recognize our neighbor in the face of the enemy who offers us a hand. I need help. Will I allow my enemy to provide it? Is Dad my enemy, or is he my neighbor as much as Angie is? Having no idea how to offer Dad compassion, and wondering if I really want to, do I just turn my head and walk on by? In Jesus's parable, the religious professionals ignore the man in the ditch. Is that who I am?

In the short term, this seems like a lot of trouble. Perhaps life would be easier if I simply moved into isolation or developed relationships that cost little and led to the accomplishment of personal goals. I'm working hard on some personal goals, some that take me into a different land. In retirement, I have entered the Solstice MFA in Creative Writing. School at this stage of my life is a great adventure, and I'm now at my first-semester writing residency at Pine Manor College in Boston. My days are full of new learning, new people, exciting challenges, and homework. It all begins around eight in the morning and for me lasts until ten at night.

The first night I fall into bed exhausted. When the phone rings around midnight, it's like a dream. I have trouble moving and struggle to find my cell phone under the papers on the end table. It's Angie, sobbing so deeply I can only understand a small portion of what she is saying. It's three hours later here than in Tucson. I listen and have no idea how to respond. She is distraught over the idea that after 15 years her husband would leave. I want to say something profound, but I can't think of any profound thing to say. I finally decide that profundity is not to be found in the space between the fog of exhaustion and compassion. I'm not very profound anyway. I listen. That seems to be good enough.

She calls back the following night, wild with worry over how this will affect her kids. A call every night, I doze off in an afternoon class. I am sorry she has this agony. I am glad she shares it with me. My gratitude is not nobility. I get to do something measurable even if it is just holding the phone and chanting, "Uh huh." I decide that I will do everything in my power to support my friend and her children even when I have no idea what that means.

In my professional life, people come to me for answers. I am a highly skilled, intuitive problem solver. Not so here. The gravity of each decision weighs heavily on my conscience. After her long, late-night cry, all I know to do is to offer a reminder that I am here, Ann is here; we will do what needs to be done. Acceptance, without a clear view of the future, seems be driven firmly into the ground next to each marker on the pathway to peace. In this case, a reminder that it may be enough to say I'm simply here. I can help with the kids. I cannot ease her pain.

When it comes to Dad, I would like to be supportive. Yet I understand why he doesn't want it, and offer a welcome sigh of relief. When I look at Jesus's parable, he encourages what can only be considered as preferential treatment of our enemies. Is Dad my enemy? If he is, and I am following Jesus, I'll tell him yes when he asks for help. He has not asked yet. My head hurts as I say to myself, I hope he invites me to become a better person. But I hope he does.

Learning to allow the love of God to lead me to a new way of loving my neighbor is not only represented by moments of interruption, but it comes alive in the design of the flow of daily life. Sunday provides the clearest picture of this.

For the last fifteen years on Sunday morning, my pattern has been to get out of bed at 4:00 a.m. After bathing and dressing, I would be the first customer at my neighborhood Starbucks. They open at 5:00 a.m. The barista would smile and have a drink and a pastry on the counter by the time I walked through the door. She would joyfully announce, "We have your order." This was fun for me. I did not intend to order the same thing each time, and she did not place a consistent order on the counter. It was always a surprise for me, though never for her. Joyfully, I would announce, "Wow. You remembered my order. Thanks." As her face brightly beamed goodbye, I would go to the car, take a sip of the drink and a peek in the bag to see what she had given me. It was a nice way to begin the day. This ritual would send me to my office to prepare for three worship services and often an additional event or two. It is an intense day. There are no breaks, no chances to let down my guard, and it seems as if every word, each nod of the head, is valued and evaluated.

After I retired, Ann and I began to imagine a day without this intensity and a new set of Sunday morning rituals. We would rise early for a walk, go to breakfast, and then attend the late service at church. I would assist when asked, be a liturgist, and preach from time to time, maybe teach a class. If we overslept, we would walk in the afternoon.

This is not how it has turned out. Dad moved out and filed for divorce. Angie is the pastor and works on Sunday morning. She needs help with the children. We have been invited. Every other week we leave our house at 7:00 a.m. and drive to Angie's house to wake the kids, get them bathed and dressed. Sometimes we also pick up our eleven-year-old grandson, JT, or his toddler sister, Victoria. When JT and Victoria come, we take two cars so that there will be enough seat belts. I had planned to sell my car and buy a pickup truck: two seat belts. Ann is suggesting that I sell it so that we can buy a minivan and the seven seat belts that would come with it.

When our kids were little and we lived in Alaska, I was the pastor and was never around to get them ready for church. The final act of getting three of them in snowsuits, boots, mittens, and hats, was a daunting, domestic adventure. Getting them to keep all of this on while Ann herded them to the car and into seat belts and car seats could be disheartening; the very real possibility that, as she pulled out of the driveway, someone would announce "I have to go to the bathroom!" could crush a parent's spirit. By the time I saw them, most of this pre-church drama was all over.

This second time around, I am fully involved. Ann has another set of adult hands, mine. Our new Sunday morning ritual includes a stop by Bruegger's Bagels, where everyone gets bagels, coffee, tea, milk, or apple juice. On the week they are at Dad's, they go with us to Bruegger's. Angie lives on the other side of town, so on her week we arrive bagels in hand. Both weeks we buy a latte for Angie and deliver it to her at church.

When it is Dad's week, we greet each other at the door. There is no visible tension in our relationship; we offer each other a few words of greeting, a comment or two about the kids. Still, the children are tense and anxious. Transitions are hard. This appears to be unavoidable. Disheveled in body and spirit, they often argue with each other and fight in the backseat. On occasion, we must pull over on the side of the road to help them make peace, and discuss how they will behave around their mom at church. They haven't seen her since Friday and have a difficult time understanding that this is her job; she cannot direct her attention exclusively to them. These transitions are constantly in flux, will change as the kids age, yet perhaps will never reach perfection. Sometimes I feel like one of the unnamed bystanders in Jesus's parable. Never mentioned, they must be there, wondering what to do, not willing to walk by and unsure of how to care for the wounded one in the ditch. It seems as if everyone is waving to me, calling me in, Come on, lend a hand. You know what to do, yet I am unsure of my role. I stumble forward, child in my arms.

This is how we want to spend our Sundays. We cannot imagine not attending worship. We no longer imagine attending alone. We love these children and we love their mother. We want to love their father, too, even though we are not sure how to express this love. At this point, the best I can do is to struggle to offer no judgment. This is not easy. While the pain of divorce threatens to drown the immediate, private life of the family, a pastor lives a public life. The waves of discontent wash upon the shore of a broad community. As I move toward not judging Dad, I must first admit that I do. I practice abandoning my judgment of Dad over and over. The problem is me, not him. I am responsible for my life, my heart, and can control no one else's. Some days I'm not convinced that I can control mine.

A life without these kinds of struggle doesn't seem like much of a life to me. Jesus makes it clear that we come fully to life when our relationship with God is visible in our relationship to others—all others. So Ann, Angie, Addison, Jackson, Brendan, surrogate grandparents, the community of the church, and I all practice reaching out from time to time to lift each other up. Perhaps, one day their dad and I will reach across the chasm of brokenness to lift each other up as we complete this parable in our own lives.

On that day, when I learn to set aside all resistance, this love of God will take a firm grip on my spirit and I will experience new freedom that will lead me to an unconditional love of all people. That day has not come yet, but I am working on it. Some days I do better than others. Angie and Ann do a better job of this than I do. I sometimes make a harsh, thoughtless comment about Dad. I'm expecting an ally but don't find one. I never do this in front of the children or our friends, yet Ann and Angie still don't appreciate it. Whoever is closest is quick to call me on it: "Speaking like this does not serve me well. It does not serve you well, either." They feel equally free to offer the reminder. Angie is required to do this for the health of her children. Ann is born a gentle and forgiving spirit.

My cell phone vibrates. It's Angie with a desperate tension in her voice, "Billy, can you come rescue Brendan, or the rest of us? He is out of control." At six years of age, he is not as articulate as his older brother and sister. While they are learning to express their feelings about their parents' divorce, Brendan's frustration erupts. Tension boils beneath the surface of his young life, and then, when it explodes, he doesn't know what to say or do. So he throws things. I find him locked in the bathroom. He has been throwing things, and he is hiding. Even in despair he is a funny kid.

"Brendan, you've gotta come out," I say.

"A guy ought to have privacy to take care of his private business," he responds.

"Thirty minutes is plenty of time."

He petulantly exits his hideout, gives me a harsh look, and then without being asked he heads for my car. We climb in the car and drive to my house where we sit around, read books, tell stories. I wait for him to relax. It doesn't take long. I suggest the quiet game. "One, two, three, go." Within five minutes he is in a deep sleep, undisturbed by all the emotions he doesn't know how to express, the lava cooling on the slopes of his life.

A week later, late in the afternoon on Thanksgiving, he and I go to the mall to see The Penguins of Madagascar. As we are driving, he asks, "Hey, Billy. Are we going to the movie together because I am in trouble or because you just like to hang out with me?"

"It's all fun today," I say.

"That's what I thought. I'm glad."

"Me too, buddy."

One night when they are at our house for supper, I ask Brendan if he would like to offer the prayer before the meal. 'Dear God' is followed by a long silence. Finally, he looks at me and says, "Hey, Billy. I got nothing." I know exactly what he means, and I tell him so. "Sometimes you just got nothing. It's okay, you'll have something later."

There are days when we all 'got nothing'. On those days, most of all the love of God leads us to the love of our neighbor, and if we are lucky we find some concrete expression of compassion.

I consider these things as I climb out of my windshield-smudged car, towel in hand, and reach for the windshield. Then I change my mind. Stopping to look at them more carefully, I imagine my little buddy walking up and across the windshield as he mounts the roof of the car. Surely, he wants to stand higher than everyone else as he watches them set up the tent in their makeshift camp. He'd imagine himself as supervisor. Perhaps for a moment, he felt some small joy. I decide not to remove the disruptive smudges of his little feet from my life. I am glad to have them blur my eyesight, even as they add clarity to my vision for my life.

The love of God leads somewhere. Perhaps it leads us to the foreign land where God is not easily recognized. There we must figure out how to love our neighbor in a new way and in a new place each time. This is hard. Loving my neighbor takes time and energy. While I worry about this occasionally, my concerns are relieved as I look at the world through my smudged windshield and I joyfully embrace the love of my neighbor that rises out of the love of God. I believe this love will lead to repentance: a turning from self-indulgence to a life in which I continually remove the barriers that surround me, creating a larger world in which I live and breathe and find my being. I am learning to be content to live with my friend through her divorce and into her new life. Where will it lead her? What will be her new land? How will she learn a new way to be a pastor, mother, friend?

I don't have to understand.

"How can we sing the Lord's song in a foreign land?"

As I drive away, the light filters through the smudges on my windshield. I see more clearly than ever as I look through the haze.

You Saved My Life!

I thought she was dead. As I turned the corner around mile forty-two of the 100-mile run, the woman lay in the trail, fully exposed to the sun. Though shade covered the path just a few feet away, she was still, unmoving. Dead or alive, this was going to take a long time. She could not be left on her own.

I approached and asked if I could touch her. She was nonresponsive. I had been a firefighter and an ETT (Emergency Trauma Technician) in rural Alaska years ago. Drawing on deep memory, I began an assessment. Her skin was dry and cool to the touch. In the world around us, the temperature was over 100 degrees. That meant she was so dehydrated she could not sweat. I checked her pulse; she began to move. Explaining everything I was doing, I got behind her, lifted her head, placed my arms under her armpits, and dragged her into the shade. I had filled my water bottles at the last aid station and hers were full. Apparently, she had not been drinking at all. Wetting a bandana, I tried to help her cool off. As she began to move around and even speak a little, I told her we had to go. We were on a single-track trail, so no one was going to drive by. Three long miles away, the next aid station housed help. We had no choice; we had to walk. I convinced her to eat and drink a bit. She immediately threw up, and I insisted she take a GU. GU is pudding-consistency carbohydrate fuel used by most ultrarunners. It can be quite renewing and easy on the stomach. After several tries she kept some down. I helped her to her feet and brushed the debris off her arms and legs. We began to stumble down the trail, covering those long miles with a staggering slowness that grew more threatening with every minute.

The three miles took almost three hours. We would stumble forward a few steps and then sit on a rock. Her eyes were glazed over and expressionless. She stared into nothingness, on the edge of surrender. I did my best to keep her talking, hoping she would become more alert. One of the last people in the race when I found her, I had been making a comeback, passing people on the trail while recovering from my own stomach distress. By the time we reached the next aid station, I was clearly last and officially timed out. My second 100 of the summer was over and incomplete; both of them burned-out disasters. I am embarrassed to say I cared. I didn't care enough to regret helping her, but I did care more than I wanted to. It was the obsessive-compulsive, light-on-compassion caring of an ultrarunner.

This aid station was just for water, but it would do. Workers and I placed her in the back of a truck, slammed the doors, and she was off to the hospital. As I watched them disappear over a hill, I realized that I was alone. The hospital was one direction, the next aid station the other. Concern for her safety had been paramount, so they had left me to find a ride to somewhere on the course where eventually I would find Ann. A fellow in a pickup truck stopped and said, "Hey, buddy, you look awful. Want a ride?" I was saved.

Ann's plan was to meet me at various places on the course to offer encouragement. By this point, she would be worried. My driver dropped me off at the next aid station, and after a series of begged rides Ann and I found each other. Addled by heat and my own dehydration, I felt like I had failed again. Timed out twice in one summer. Everyone has an excuse.

In the ultrarunning community, a myth of selflessness overstates a somewhat self-righteous attitude. We take pride in being different from marathoners and certainly from triathletes. Our elites hang out with the also-rans. We offer genuine congratulations to all who finish and never look down on the back of the pack. Yet on this day, at Rio Del Lago, more than one runner passed Lillie and me on the trail without inquiring about our safety or offering to help. At every turn, I expected to see someone coming back to offer assistance. Had the runners who passed us made a conscious decision to ignore us and leave us in danger? Were they so single-mindedly absorbed in their own goals that they failed to notice our obvious distress?

My friend Jerry, who was also running the race that day, had a similar experience years later in the Old Pueblo 50. While the race took place on a cold, rainy, stormy day, he helped a dangerously hypothermic runner struggle to the next aid station, virtually carrying him down the trail. Runners that he knew zoomed past, unwilling to slow down in the wet and the cold. As I have reflected on this over the years, I have wondered how often I do this in my daily life. How often do I ignore someone's distress because I am too concerned about the inconvenience it will visit upon my life? I have places to go, things to do; I live on a tight budget financially and energetically, and stopping to help could subvert much of that. Perhaps I could blame God for my frequent ultrarunning failures. Perhaps God wants me to stop! Perhaps there are Lilies everywhere!

As this particular cycle of praying leads us in the direction of peace, it takes a detour through the valley of repentance. Prayer begins with silence. Silence leads to the love of God. The love of God leads to the love of our neighbor, and now the love of our neighbor leads to repentance. How does loving my neighbor lead me to repentance? Could it be that the love of my neighbor leads to repentance because this love requires a lot of time and work that I am reluctant to give? Repentance often gets a bad rap. Sometimes when I hear the word, especially if it is spoken loudly, I have a vision of an angry, bearded, poorly dressed fellow holding a sign on a street corner; "Repent! The end is near!" If I am not careful, I can embrace the misguided idea that repentance is simply costly, negative, and filled with guilt. A deeper understanding of the word allows me to recognize the great gift of freedom and possibility it offers. The simplest meaning of repentance is to turn around. Not just to turn, but to turn and begin to move in another direction.

When Jesus announces, "Repent, the Kingdom of God is at hand!" he is announcing the beauty of possibility. I am invited to turn from the things that are hurting me, from my short-sighted view of life and to embrace something as broad, deep, wide, and all-encompassing as a worldview fashioned by turning to God. Jesus says, turn around and live your life large and full of the possibility. Repentance calls for a radical shift in thinking. In its most common New Testament usage, it is a compound word. It combines the preposition after with the verb to perceive, think, or observe. We could say that repentance means: after observation, I turn around. I could say the consequences that rose out of seeing Lillie lying in the trail dwarfed the significance of completing a running event. I turned around. Once. Throughout my life I must make this decision for repentance over and over.

After a shower and a nap at our hotel, I got up and Ann took me to find Jerry. We found him approaching the ninety-mile aid station. From there I paced him as he ran the last ten miles. At least I could help my friend finish. It felt important to accomplish some running goal.

Ultrarunning is an odd, obscure sport. While urban marathons often include tens of thousands of entrants, ultras rarely include more than a couple of hundred people. Marathons often tout flat fast courses. Ultras brag of thousands of feet in elevation gain, ascents of mountain passes, highly technical rocky descents, altitude, river crossings, and long stretches through fully exposed desert landscapes. Urban marathons tell you that there will be large crowds cheering for you along the course. In an ultra, you may run alone for hours. You can eagerly anticipate no more than tens of people to encourage you in most aid stations, and when you arrive at the finish, you hope to be greeted by your spouse or a few close friends, if they haven't given up and gone home. To be a spectator or support crew at an ultra is a sign of love… it is a long, boring day. While ultracourses come in many distances, they are all longer than 26.2 miles, the standard marathon length, thus the name ultramarathon. The most popular distances are 50 kilometers, 50 miles, 100 kilometers, and 100 miles. I ran the 50k distance of the Vail Colossal Cave 50k/50m. It was 56 kilometers long. No one thought that was odd. An extra four miles tacked onto the end of a 26.2-mile marathon would cause a riot.

Ultras attract obsessive-compulsive, highly independent people. Except for the elites of the sport, most folks find the course challenging enough. No need to waste competitive energy on others. Compete with yourself. Ultrarunners take great pride in wearing clothes that do not match, throwing up on the trail, then continuing to run. The elites of our sport often hang out around the finish line for hours to greet the citizen runners who will never win but who give their all just to cover the distance. I remember standing at the starting line of the Old Pueblo 50 Mile Endurance Run when my friend Mike turned to me and said, "This is going to take all day. It's going to be really hard, it will hurt a lot, and we are not going to win." Everyone within earshot of this declaration responded with an affirmative laugh.

These are some common ultrarunning affirmations: "It's like fun, only different."

"Suffering is pain leaving your body."

"It never always gets worse."

"We were blowing past rocks and trees as if they were standing still."

"Relentless forward motion."

"Pain is temporary. Glory lasts."

"Be stronger than your excuses."

I once entered the Iditasport, now known as the Susitna 100. It is 100 miles through the interior of Alaska in February. You can run, ski, snowshoe, or bike. All participants are required to carry survival gear, and there are only four checkpoints, so even though the course is marked you must be capable of finding your own way. The t-shirts used to say Cowards Don't Show and the Weak Die until one year two skiers were lost for over a day, and folks began to think that perhaps they had died. Few wanted to wear the shirt when the announcement of impending death felt like a real possibility.

It's a hard sport. People rarely die but as in any sport, it can happen. The Javelina Jundred 100 Mile Endurance Run registration application requires you to sign a release acknowledging:

"I know that running on trails poses many hazards, not limited to falls, bad weather, rockslides, getting lost, wild animal attack, and generally dangerous conditions. I am entering this event with full knowledge that I could easily be hurt or face life-threatening injuries. I fully assume all risks of injury, illness, or death."

In an ultra, there are aid stations along the way. These are places where you can replenish your supplies, fill water bottles, pick up food, and sometimes change shirts or socks or attend to medical needs. They can be comforting and therefore often have signs with reminders such as:

"Beware the chair."

"No one ever finished sitting down."

In a warm cabin on the Iditasport course, where there was soup and coffee inside while the wind blew at twenty degrees below zero outside, there hung a banner, "Where Iditasport Dreams Come to Die."

At many aid stations, time goals must be met. It is not unusual for a 100-mile event to have a DNF (Did Not Finish) rate of 35-40 percent. Some of the more difficult races have occasional DNF rates over 50 percent, and these are events for which you must qualify. A runner must leave the aid station before these times. If you don't make it, you are 'timed out'. In an unceremonious, matter-of-fact manner, your identification band is clipped from your wrist, you are pulled from the race, and after months and sometimes years of training, your dreams are dashed. I had timed out of the Kettle Moraine 100 earlier in the summer. Discouragement dominated my running imagination as I was looking for a way to salvage months of training when my friend Jerry suggested we give it a try at Rio del Lago. Rio did not require qualifying times, and although it was hard, and one hundred miles is always a long way to run and many starters would not finish, it was considered a good place to accomplish your first one hundred-mile finish. For me, it was my first 100 in a long time. I timed out there, too, pulling Lillie up a hill.

You might say that I am an ultra-liver. Once I have turned my head in a particular direction, it becomes exceptionally difficult for me to turn around. A crisis is often required to remind me that life is full of options. God is possibility.

The next fall, still nursing the discouragement of a two-failure summer, Jerry and I were operating an aid station at the Javelina Jundred 100 Mile Endurance Run. Beyond the distance itself, this well-organized event has one major challenge: the desert sun. It's run in October, so while the temperatures are not really hot, the direct sun is relentless. There is not one step taken in the shade. This makes each aid station unusually important. The workers must closely observe the runners to be sure they are drinking enough and paying attention to electrolyte replacement. We were careful to speak to everyone who passed through. I was doing my job and enjoying it when I saw a woman who had passed through our aid station coming back. She looked at me and said, "You saved my life!"

All I knew was that she was going the wrong way. I laughed and said, "No, I did not save your life. Now get out of here."

Her second loop of six fifteen-mile loops, plus one of ten made this far too early in the day for her to feel bad, or for her thinking to be muddled by heat or nutritional depletion. All of those things can happen later in the day, and they often happen early during the second morning of an event that can last up to thirty hours. But not yet. She did not look familiar to me and yet she was insistent in her declaration.

"No, I can't go. Please, I think about you all the time. I have to know who you are."

I was getting a bit uncomfortable. This seemed to be moving beyond a joke. "Look," I said, "I don't know you, and I did not save your life. Now you've got to get out of here or you will get behind. Go."

"Last year, were you at Rio Del Lago?"

"Yes."

"I'm Lillie, the woman you found on the trail. You saved my life."

My heart rate increased as I stepped out from behind the table to meet her outstretched arms. It was as if we were old friends. My eyes began to swell with tears as I thought of that afternoon at Rio del Lago, when I had turned around.

She and I embraced long and hard and vigorously kissed each other's cheeks, laughing with joy. "I wondered if you were okay," I said. "How did you know it was me?"

"One day I was watching A Race for the Soul, and when you spoke I recognized your voice and I knew it was you, but I could not find anyone who knew your name. Then today, when I heard your voice, I knew again it was you. It echoes in my head all the time."

A Race for the Soul is a documentary about the Western States 100, in which I make a brief appearance. At an aid station, I go down a row of people who are my crew. I kiss Ann, our daughter Sara, my niece Mary Beth, and my PT friend Kristin, as I tell them I love them. At the last moment, I look up to see the camera. I smile and speak to the cameraman, "I love you, too!" Many ultrarunners watch this documentary, and for a number of years people referred to me as 'the love guy'.

"We'll talk later. Now really, you need to go."

She smiled, said, "I love you, too," and disappeared down the trail.

Later in the day as she passed through our aid station again, we exchanged names and promised to search for each other on Facebook. Lillie was in her mid-twenties, about the same age as my daughter. I was in my mid-fifties. We were both ultrarunners.

Lillie and I have not seen each other since that day at the Javelina Jundred. My volunteer shift at the aid station was up, and I was on my way home long before she timed out once again, yet we have developed a friendship that is fulfilling for both of us. The only way we have communicated is through instant messaging (private messages), Facebook, and email. Our friendship began cautiously enough. We each recounted our memory of that day at Rio Del Lago. It had been a stressful situation, and both of us had some gaps in our memory. She filled her memory gaps with overstated acts of heroism performed by a mysterious man with a distinctive voice who would not let her die. Mine were more mundane. They mostly consisted of a long slog carrying a barely conscious young woman up a hilly trail.

In time, we began to probe deeper into the possibilities of our friendship. After a lifetime of terrible encounters with Christians and especially clergy, she found the possibility of a long-distance friendship with me, an older Christian pastor, worthy of guarded exploration. She had been judged and abused by family and church and wanted to explore questions of faith from the safety of distance and the obscurity of an invisible friend. We began to inquire about each other's lives in a quite specific manner.

When one of my closest friends died by suicide, our unusual friendship began in earnest. Lillie played an unexpected role. She boldly asked questions others ignored. Perhaps protected by the lack of shared history and limited knowledge of each other that predated that day at Rio del Lago, she asked if I felt a sense of guilt or responsibility for his death. Had I ever considered suicide? How seriously did I take my responsibility to care for his wife and others who had loved him? Did I believe he had still loved me? When I answered, she probed deeper and challenged the places where I was avoidant. Because she was the only person with whom I had spoken of his death, for whom I felt no responsibility to offer comfort, I was free to tell the unself-conscious truth with no thought to consequences. I was not her pastor; we did not share a mutual history with my friend or our families. She was simply compassionately curious, allowing me to explore my thoughts and feelings without feeling protective of either of us.

I found out that she was on her own; she wanted to go to school so badly and was so radically independent that for one semester she lived in a tent, hiding in the woods behind her university campus, bathing in the student athletic facility, walking back and forth several miles each day so that she had money to pay her tuition without incurring unreasonable debt. That semester, she completed her degree with such success that she was accepted to a PhD program in organic chemistry.

Sometimes, in my imagination I see her body lying on the trail. I cannot imagine walking past someone in such obvious distress, but I suppose I often do. I want to love my neighbor as myself. This is not my first instinct. Turning around reveals one of the ways I step into God's possibilities for a new life. Turning around also created a place where Lillie could speak to me and I was not the pastor. She felt free to probe with her unself-conscious curiosity in ways most others would not.

Sometimes I wonder if I would I have completed Rio Del Lago had I not stopped to help Lillie. I don't know. I do know that whether I finished or not would not have mattered much.

Stopping with Lillie mattered. Did I save her life that day on the trail? Would someone else have stopped if I hadn't? Perhaps. However, I'm glad it was me. I am grateful that in her distress she offered me the opportunity to turn around, with observation. To look beyond myself and take another step into the possibility of a new life.

Live Until You Die

As I cradled my head in my hands, I felt like a knife had broken my sternum, piercing my chest. I didn't even notice the gray, icy water seeping through my shorts until I stood up to walk and found my buttocks soaked. What was happening?

All through April, I had experienced intermittent chest pain while running. I would run through my Anchorage, Alaska, neighborhood. After seven minutes, it would start. I would slow down to a walk, and it would go away. It would not return during that run. What did this mean?

Mount St. Augustine had been erupting and the snow housed layers of volcanic ash. As snow melted, the ash blew free. I explained the frequent chest discomfort as a bad cold aggravated by volcanic ash, a uniquely Alaskan form of denial.

As I stood to walk home, the icy, gray water that had soaked through my shorts dripped down my legs; I became chilled. April in south central Alaska is not terribly cold, but the world is wet. It's still hard to stay warm. Six months of snow melts in a few weeks; drains are frozen; water has nowhere to drain. It pools over the earth, waiting to be soaked into your shoes, socks, or your running shorts. I found myself in denial about the chest pain but not about the threat of my wet clothes and freezing skin. In my mind, this added up to a rough morning.

I went home, showered, and drove to my office. I did not mention the incident to Ann, not yet. I am not a man of few words. Part of my job is to be articulate about faith and life's most significant issues, but today, I had nothing to say.

As I arrived in my office I was developing a strong urge to confirm one thing: that nothing was seriously wrong. I shut the door and got out the phone book. This was 1990, pre-Internet, and I had not seen a doctor in a long time. My thinking was not very clear as I lifted the big, bulky Yellow Pages book and opened it on my desk. Even though my thought process was a bit jumbled, I knew that I wanted to find a non-surgeon physician with a cardiac specialty. I opened the Yellow Pages to Physicians and scanned the pages. Two doctors in the Anchorage phone book met my criteria. I knew one of them. I called the other one and told the receptionist my story.

"It would be best if you went to the emergency room," she said. "No, I feel fine now. I really don't want to do that."

"Well, we don't have any openings today."

"I need your help. If you don't have any openings, perhaps I will just come and sit in your lobby until someone can help me."

"Oh my," she sighed, "Thank you for not doing that. I'll check with the doctor and call you back within the hour."

I hung up the phone and told the church office manager I would be back in a few minutes. I got in my car, drove to Wendy's and ordered a double bacon cheeseburger, a large order of fries, and a Frosty. While stuck between believing nothing was wrong and an uncertain future, I had a premonition that my life was going to change. I savored every bite. Would I ever eat like this again? Fatty, greasy, salty, and so large I had to push it flat to get in into my mouth?

It was to be the last hamburger of my life.

The doctor's receptionist called back. She assured me that their office wanted to help and that if I came in an hour, and was willing to wait, the doctor would find a way to work me into his schedule. As I got in my car and went to meet Dr. Sherman Beacham, I noticed that my hands were trembling. This was the first sign that my outward denial was surrendering to the obvious truth.

On that morning Dr. Beacham and the nurses helped me remove my shirt. They shaved my chest and hooked up electrodes. Following the Bruce protocol, the treadmill begins flat and slow, barely moving. Every three minutes it speeds up and increases its incline. The goal is to measure your heart function in a timely and efficient manner. After about three minutes the nurse asked in a voice that failed to mask her alarm, "How do you feel? Are you in a lot of pain?"

"No," I replied, "no pain at all."

As I fought the urge to run out of the room, I wanted to scream, Of course there is no pain. Do you know who I am? I'm still young, living a strong, vigorous life. This is just a mistake. I shouldn't be here.

In another couple of minutes, she asked again. Well, okay, I acknowledged a modest but rising discomfort as she and Dr. Beacham moved me from the treadmill, laid me on an examination table, placed nitroglycerin under my tongue, and asked me not to move. It was at this point that I realized that I was not simply having a bad day. This really was going to change my life. It was as if I could feel the water from my icy, wet, long discarded, morning running shorts dripping down the back of my legs once again. The nurse covered me in a blanket as I began to shiver.

Dr. Beacham's office was adjacent to Humana Hospital.

"Why don't we just walk over and check you into the hospital?"

"I don't know. Do you think I am going to die today?"

"Probably not, but why take that chance?"

What chance? I thought. I'm young. A runner, skier, cyclist, climber, stronger than the average guy. I'm not gonna die and I don't need your help! Yet I obviously did, and even I knew it.

Foolish as it was, I decided not to go, not yet. Thinking about my wife, Ann, and our three little children, it seemed important to me to go home and talk to them before I did anything as dramatic as checking into the hospital. They didn't even know I had gone to the doctor. I sat on the edge of the examining table thinking while the doctor's office made an appointment with another physician who would perform an angiogram in a couple of days.

Here's how denial worked for me. I drove to my office. I went back to work. That night I taught Disciple Bible Study at Anchor Park United Methodist Church, where I was pastor. I got home about 9:00 p.m. and only then, hours after the fact, did I tell Ann about my experience. On numerous occasions, Ann and I have tried to reconstruct the conversation we had that night. We cannot do it. We were in shock, and the things that were primary in the conversation simply did not make sense to us.

Heart disease? How was that possible?

The next morning, still feeling as if I was stuck in the foggy awakening of a bad dream, I kept my appointment with Dr. Sonneborn, another kind, gray-haired yet much younger man who introduced himself and invited me into his office. He looked at the reports from Dr. Beacham; I had delivered them myself. With a look of questioning calm, he asked, "Mr. Still, are you married?"

"Yes," I replied.

"Are you and your wife estranged?"

"No, not at all. Why do you ask?"

"Because this is a very serious matter that involves some risk and will affect the rest of your life. Unless you have some reason to exclude her, your wife should be a part of this conversation. I'll leave the room so you can call her and ask her to join us. Let the receptionist know when she arrives and we will talk then."

He left the room. I felt very alone.

Once again I put my elbows on my knees and cradled my head between my hands as I wondered at the cold chill that swept up and down my spine and over my spirit. Until this point I had considered this a stop at the doctor's office on the way to my own office. I had said to Ann, "I'll call you when I get to church and let you know what he said." When I called Ann, I simply said, "Dr. Sonneborn wants you to be here."

"Do you want me to be there?"

I tried to think of some way to answer her without sounding alarmed. I failed. "Yes, hurry please."

Our house was less than ten minutes away from Providence Hospital, but it seemed like an eternity as I sat and waited. The serious nature of this event became clearer by the minute. Except for childbirth, or visiting parishioners, neither of us had ever been in a hospital before. Now here we sat, waiting for a cardiologist in an office in a hospital wing, preparing to check in, discussing the next steps in understanding this disease. To this point, Ann and I had no in-depth discussions about anything, death, dying, hospitals, the kids…we simply did not know what to say.

The next day I had an angiogram. This interventional catheterization allowed the physician to see the blockage in the coronary artery so an informed decision could be made about the next level of treatment. Information filtered in even though I was unable to process much of it.

119

The fog of the mild anesthesia made it impossible to focus on the doctor's voice. I remember the wave of sleep washing over me, and then, I was awake and Ann was beside me. We asked the same questions over and over, unable to process the answers. Perhaps they told us everything at once, but we had to hear it multiple times before we could process it.

I learned later that Dr. Sonneborn exited the cath lab and came to the waiting room to speak to Ann and some friends who were waiting with her. He told her that up to 98 percent of my left anterior descending artery (LAD) was blocked with plaque and that this large artery was the primary source of blood to the heart. How had I avoided a heart attack? Who has a 98 percent blockage and no heart attack? Me. My excellent physical condition had masked many of the symptoms of the disease. My body had developed a series of vessels that provided corollary circulation. This had been building up for a long time. The motivation to live an active, vigorous life caused me to live beyond any reasonable physical expectations. Perhaps I really was invincible and this was just some weird mistake?

Foolish thoughts.

I could hide from my heart no more. Something had to be done.

In consultation with Dr. Beacham, Ann and I agreed that the best path was to have an angioplasty. This procedure is invasive in the same way as the angiogram: a balloon is inflated that packs the plaque against the side of the artery. About 30 percent of the time it is ineffective within six months. The younger and otherwise healthier you are, the less likely this is to work. Flexible arteries tend to move back into their old shape. Oddly enough, though my high level of fitness certainly worked in my favor, it also decreased the chances of success with this particular procedure.

We scheduled the procedure. I had little to lose.

While I lay in my hospital bed waiting for the next day, all I thought was, Thank you. It was not a particularly noble thought; however, it was real. At that point no one had asked about money. We had insurance. Many people had offered support to our children and Ann. I was not worried about my job or the quality of medical care. Though my imagination soared back and forth from denial to despair, acceptance was the only helpful place to land. Really, I was powerless. In this moment there was nothing for me to do but sit back, embrace my situation, and say thank you. So I did.

Ann went home early that night to talk with our children. Chris was 10, Joe 7, and Sara 3. As they talked, Chris looked Ann straight in the eyes and asked, "Is Dad going to die?"

"No," Ann said. "Everyone dies someday, but your dad is not going to die from this."

"How do you know? Could he die?"

Ann looked at all of them, then told them the truth. "Probably your dad will be fine, but yes, he could die."

Thus came the barrage of childlike questions. They are generally direct, straight forward, and can seem a bit cold, but these questions are real for children.

"If Dad dies, where will we live?"

"Who will take care of us?"

"How will we get to school?"

"How will we get enough money?"

"Mom, you don't ski. Who will take us skiing?"

As Ann listened to these questions, she reassured our children that they would be fine. Even if the worst happened, they had plenty of family, friends, and insurance to bridge the immediate financial gap. But after the kids went to bed, Ann rehearsed these questions in her imagination, wondering at her own answers. *How will we get enough money?* Although she had a teaching degree, she had not taught in quite a while, and she realized that teaching was not how she wanted to spend her life. She decided that night: no matter what happened to me, she was going back to school.

This life adventure began mid-April, two weeks after Easter. The procedure went fine. Within five days, I was running again. Even the doctors involved seemed eager to embrace that fact. They were eager for me to run and bike. Most of their patients were older, heavier, out of shape, and oddly enough, didn't seem interested in finding new ways to live. I became their curiosity. It was all good, as if nothing had happened.

But for me denial was no longer the helpful tool it once was. In my own imagination I became an anxious curiosity. Each time I felt a twinge in my chest, I wondered, *Is this a muscle pull, a stitch because I am out of breath, a sign that I am out of shape and should work harder, or is this a return of my blocked arteries?*

On the fourth of July, my anxiety is confirmed. After a cookout with our friends, we play soccer in a field. As I run for the ball, a sharp feeling stabs my chest. I slow down, and it goes away. I speed up; it returns. The next day, I see Dr. Beacham, and we begin the process again. Angioplasty number two.

We fall into the arms of false hope. We relax. This one will work. Then, in another three months, the pain returns and portends procedure number three. While on my morning run, on the sidewalk in our neighborhood beside Lake Otis Parkway, I am staggered by piercing in my chest.

Now we know, angioplasty is not the answer. We are already 0 for 2.

I have a lot of questions. The four-year survival rate is the same for medication, angioplasty, or coronary artery bypass. I want to do the most conservative thing possible. That being said, the most conservative response provides the greatest short-term risk of a heart attack or stroke. On the other end of the spectrum, a bypass can put some parenthesis around your life. They don't last forever, and I am only thirty-seven years old.

"Let's take a while to think and do research," Dr. Beacham says. "Take it easy and don't run until we get this figured out."

While I had developed great trust in his judgment, I know the clock is ticking loudly while we decide what to do. Anxiety is no longer a houseguest. She moves in and sets up housekeeping. Although I didn't realize it at the time, I am confident that my stress level caused me to be a difficult husband and father. I think I did a better job of masking my anxiety at work. At least I hope I did. Snapping at Ann and the children is not okay, but they are far more likely to tolerate this temporary snarkiness than the office manager, choir director, associate pastor, or custodian. My anxiety level is high as I stare at the phone, waiting for a call, wondering if the next one will be Dr. Beacham, calling with a plan that's going to save my life. Or not.

The next week, as I sit at my desk early in the morning, trying unsuccessfully to focus on the day's task, the phone finally rings. Dr. Beacham asks, "Can you go to San Francisco this week?"

This week? Can Ann get away? Who will care for the kids? What about preparing for church on Sunday? Can we afford it? How long will we be gone? A multitude of practical questions riffle quickly through my head all pointing toward the same destination. Without resolving any of them, I simply say, "Sure."

Then it occurs to me to ask what I should have asked first, "Why?"

He explains that a new procedure, rotational atherectomy, is being developed. Though invasive in the same manner as angioplasty, it will actually remove the plaque that clogged my artery. The developer of this procedure is demonstrating it for the American College of Cardiac Surgeons, and he is looking for a patient like me. As Ann and I discuss this possibility, we acknowledge that we are eager to move ahead. At the same time, we admit it: we both have anxiety over the experimental nature of the procedure. While it has been performed on femoral arteries, I will be among the first to have this procedure performed on a LAD.

Then, our insurance company informed us that they had denied payment. After a brief crisis, Dr. Beacham convinces the researchers to operate for free. Our expenses are limited to travel and hotel cost. In the end, the only reason to refuse would be fear of this new procedure.

I do not make decisions based on fear, but this time I do think to ask,

"Dr. Beacham, if it were you or your wife, would you go?"

"Without a doubt. Your only remaining choice is a bypass. At your tender age we want to avoid that. If this doesn't work, we can always do that later."

I hang up the phone. Ann and I turn to each other, and she knows already. We say together, "The children! Who will take care of the children?"

I call my mother in Jackson, Mississippi. She is on a plane for Anchorage, and her own adventure, the next day. Shortly after she arrives, Ann and I board another plane.

One more try.

In the San Francisco airport, as we walked to the luggage carousel, I found it humiliating to ask Ann to slow down. My chest hurt if I walked too fast. Is this my imagination? Whatever it was, it scared me.

When we arrived at our hotel, we called to see if all was well. "Oh honey, it's perfect, being here with your lovely children." I could hear a "but" coming. "Yes?"

"It snowed a foot last night. I've never driven in snow. I don't know how I will get them to school, or me to the grocery, or…" her voice cracks.

I realized my southern Mississippi born-and-bred mother was in a serious position. We had simply left town without arranging any support for my mom, who fearlessly engaged the sub-arctic cold on behalf of us and her grandchildren. Could we be that thoughtless? Apparently so! I called my associate and good friend David. We had both grown up in Jackson, Mississippi. We were pastors at the same church in Anchorage, and he had known my mother for decades.

I took a hard-won breath. "David, I don't have much energy left. Will you deal with this? Will you help my mom? And by the way, I forgot to ask, will you do my job for a while?"

Within hours, neighbors were plowing snow, arranging schedules to drive the kids, taking my mom to the grocery, delivering meals, and more.

The research surgeon is Dr. Matthew Selmon. On the day before the procedure we are in his office when I ask, "What will you and the nurses say to each other when you roll me out of the operating room?"

"What do you mean?"

"I want to know if will you say, 'Poor guy, does he know he's going to die?' or will you say, 'Well, we saved another life?'"

He smiled and said, "You could be back here in a year and a half. If so, we will help you, but clearly that will be bad news. You will surely need some kind of intervention in another ten years or less. Who knows what we will know by then? Everyone dies of something. You just happen to know what yours is. In all likelihood, some day you will die of heart disease unless you get hit by a truck first. Either of those could be many years away."

All of my life, I considered myself invincible. Growing up, I was not a good athlete and as an adult I have never been unusually strong, yet I am overwhelmingly persistent, and most of the time I lack the fear gene. I just don't become afraid quickly or easily. It rarely occurs to me to anticipate an accident, and I rarely think that I will be seriously hurt. When I do have that thought, my typical response is to gather my bearings and then push ahead.

Today it's pretty clear that my persistence isn't enough. I am not in control. Fear nibbles at the edges of my psyche. I pay attention. And for the first time, Ann reflects more deeply on her conversations with the kids. We are forced to take seriously her need to think of how they will manage if I am not around to help. When the next semester begins at the University of Alaska, Anchorage, Ann will be an accounting student.

Three nights later, Ann and I were holed up in a hotel room in Bodega Bay, California. Dr. Selmon had asked us to stay in the area for a few days, in case there were complications. It really was a dark and stormy night. We built a fire in the fireplace, drew back the blinds, and watched a massive storm sweep across the bay, lashing sheets of rain into the sliding glass door. Our supper would remain uneaten on a table. The level of exhaustion we experienced was too deep to be moderated by food. We sat, stunned and lost.

I found myself grappling with the relationship between my faith, my disease, and these marvelous, yet seemingly endless medical interventions. I was not afraid of pain or death, and my faith was not at risk, yet I longed for ways to deepen this faith as I embraced the struggle of the moment. I had no desire to move rapidly ahead. There was nothing in me insisting on a quick resolution to this tension. Everything in me longed for a guide who would sit with me, acknowledge the tension, and bless the struggle, so—as is my habit in such times—I picked up a book and began to read.

The Wilderness Essays of John Muir.

Many traditional Christian authors write with a specific purpose: to convince, to explain, or to defend the faith. These authors are plentiful and would be quick to throw light on my dilemma. They might even be helpful, but on this night, none of that felt necessary or important.

I was not on a quest for answers but rather a grounding that would allow me to frame the questions. How would I recognize and welcome God, the ground of our being, when the ground seemed to be crumbling beneath me? Where would I find a guide who would stand beside me, raising a voice in a dissonant longing to embrace life's questions, while not insisting upon answers? What does it mean to seek God alive in the mayhem?

Beyond those close friends who have nurtured my life over time, I find myself drawn to writers who fearlessly echo this quest, who embrace questions of faith that rise out of the organic structure of our daily lives, and are not invested in the disciplines of academic argument or even deep inspiration.

From that place beside the roaring fire and next to the window that protected us from the storm, I looked at the mystery of faith and did not quite know what to think, or feel. I was safe from the storm, and until this illness had struck, my life had been exceeding all reasonable expectations.

My wife was a marvelous person who loved me and shared a vigorous curiosity of the world. We had three healthy, well-adjusted, adventuresome children. I had a challenging job coupled with time for adventure. Even faced with this illness, I had good insurance and no substantive financial worries. Our community was compassionate and caring, so my job was not at risk. While wondering about the connection between this life, a hazardous health crisis, and the mystery of faith that ties all things together, there was no hunger in my soul for large theological constructs that explain why disaster strikes people of faith, nor for a defense of God's love in a place where it might be questioned.

Still, I eagerly turned to my old friend John Muir; a writer who had accepted the freedom to stand at the crossroads of life and faith. "One learns that the world, though made, is yet being made; that this is still the morning of creation; that mountains long conceived are now being born, channels traced for coming rivers, basins hollowed for lakes..."

And I would add faith, long conceived, is also always being born. It is indeed the morning of creation. Looking out the window, Muir in hand, lost in thought, and entranced by the swirling tempest, I noticed two cyclists stuck in the storm, heads down, peddling into the wind, and I came to the crux of my questioning: I wondered if I would be granted the privilege to enter into that kind of voluntary adventurous suffering once again.

I opened the book of Muir's essays and found myself touched deep in my soul as I read his reflections on destruction. "What we, in faithless ignorance call destruction, is God alive in creation." Muir goes on to remind us once again, "It is still the morning of creation."

I began to wonder if God was creating something new in me, or out of me.

When John Muir stood at the base of Yosemite Falls, he looked up and said, "What a glorious place for a mountaineer to die." While I do not believe Muir wanted to die, I do believe he longed to recognize the glory of the place where he was able to live. Embracing this beauty would surely add meaning to his inevitable death.

Thinking of Muir, I remember my friend Rick, who during the previous six months had often stopped by my office. Recognizing my gradual slide into depression, he had decided to become my encourager. Several times a week he parked his truck by the front door of the church and dashed in. Ignoring the receptionist who was tasked with screening my guests, he pushed open the door to my office, came barnstorming in, leaned across my desk, his massive smile dominating his face and his heart. And then he said, "Billy, live until you die, man. Live until you die."

Just a few months later, Rick, newly married, a pilot, and bear guide, crashed his Cessna 180 into a mountainside. He was fully alive until the moment of his death.

Rick and Muir remind me: I am on a mission to live, fully alive until I die. I want to be ready to climb on my bike and ride into the storm, but I'm not. Not yet. My question is different. Who am I now, and how do I live my life in this diminished state? Am I noble enough to live well, as a follower of Jesus, a loving husband and father, a faithful pastor and friend, if I lose touch with a life punctuated by physical adventure? Without this, who do I become?

The surgeons spoke as if I had survived a train wreck. To me, it felt as if the train was falling off the track. Now I had to learn how to go home, resume my life, and enjoy it until the train jumped the tracks again. As I sat in countless waiting rooms, I looked around and realized something critical: most people did not change their lives after an experience like this. Most did not exercise, substantially alter their diet, or lose weight, and within a brief period of time most folks resumed their daily life with no serious thought to reducing stress.

I became judgmental as I observed these folks, creating imaginative scenarios that explained why I was different from them. It helped to embrace the illusion that I could once again take control of my body…my life. Yet even as I grasped for this chimera, it slipped through my hands, leaving me to wonder if I could be sure of anything.

Who was I now?

There was one assurance I could grasp. I could stack the deck in my favor. Dr. Selmon had said I would probably need another surgical intervention in no more than ten years. I was determined that when that day came, I would be able to look at my family and myself in the mirror and declare, "I have done my best to care for this gift I have been given." This would require me to better care for two things: I would care for my body and spirit in a new way, paying attention to exercise, diet, and stress management while embracing the gift of every moment. I would be required to care for my spirit in a new way, too. I wanted to identify the behaviors that had contributed to my disease, not for the purposes of blame and guilt, but so that I could take responsibility for developing new practices that would lead to a healthier life.

The primary struggle, as always, was between my desire to be in charge, to take control of my life, and at the same time to surrender my life in unquestioning trust, to God.

I realize this sounds cliché, but it's what I still want to do. Every time I run, ride my bike, step into my skis, wrestle on the floor with our kids, make love with my wife, stand in front of the church, or offer myself in friendship, I want to exist in the moment as if there is no other—not fearing the future but embracing the intensity of being in love with today.

I met with Dr. Beacham often. He agreed that taking responsibility for myself as I sought life changes was critical. While he studiously avoided presenting himself as a theologian, a therapist, nutritionist, exercise physiologist, or expert in stress management, he would help me navigate the medical world. As to the rest: I was on my own.

Ann eagerly joined me on this quest. I do not know how I could have accomplished anything if my life partner had not been an eager participant. Knowing that we needed to change, but would need to take it in small doses, we started with diet. With food.

But then there was the day we stood in the aisle at Carrs grocery in Anchorage, paralyzed.

I looked at the deli counter, at the deep-fried burritos. They would taste good and be filling, sure, but they were not on the list. What was the alternative? We were unclear. We looked at the fish, but we already had a freezer full of fresh salmon and halibut. While we pursued fresh vegetables, we couldn't help but consider how long it would take to prepare all this fresh food. Tension continued to rise. It became clear we could not struggle like this every day. I thought, *This is too hard. I can't do this three times a day. Let's surrender and get a double bacon cheeseburger.*

I began to gain a more compassionate understanding of those I had judged. We didn't buy the deep-fried burrito.

We did decide to ask Dr. John Schlife for help. Marching into Dr. Schlife's office for our first appointment, I told him my story and announced that I would be his most committed patient. "Tell me what I cannot eat, and I'll never eat it again," I boldly declared.

He laughed and suggested that was not a helpful place to start. "Let's start with what would be helpful for you to eat. Pay attention to that, and you will not be hungry. Then, after we've established some new habits, we will talk about the whys."

At his suggestion, Ann and I began to shop primarily in the produce section. We began to prepare our own food more and to purchase fewer pre-packaged foods. Burritos could be made from beans we cooked, with fillers that were fresh and not from cans. These became a lunchtime favorite. As it became clear that my cholesterol levels were tied to meat and other fatty foods, we decided not to eat meat and became pescatarians, eating fish packed with omega 3s from our own icy Alaskan waters. Salmon tacos, halibut enchiladas, and fish burgers became staples. Sweet potatoes were sliced thin, then baked with olive oil. Yes, we were required to think more about food preparation. Although it was trouble, we lost weight, felt better, and our cholesterol improved. Because this way of eating was considered odd in Alaska in the early 1990s, invitations to meals with friends declined.

Then there was the question of exercise. Dr. Schlife, an ultraathlete himself, said, "I don't think you can do much more. Perhaps you should consider doing differently." I began to chart my running and to add a long day each week. A forty-five minute to one-hour run was the daily norm. On my long day, I would run two to three times the distance of my average daily run. This led me to running ultramarathons, races longer than a marathon and most often on trails. Along with a few adventure races that were several hundred miles long, I have run over thirty fifty-mile trail races. Beyond that, running, biking, and skiing long distances renew my spirit and my mind, they relieve me of stress and help me to believe I can retake some of the control this disease has taken from my life. I will often identify a remote trail over a mountain ridge, and while I might enjoy your company, I don't need your help. I cross it alone, because I can. This brings me to life. Regaining control of my body helped me to believe that, at least for now, this disease did not have to control my life.

When it came to stress management, the only other reasonable place to look for change was work. My typical response is, "If some is good, more must be better." This had been my practice at work. I was accustomed to going to the church office early in the morning so that I could write before others arrived. Then it was my custom to work until the evening meal, head home to share that with the family and often return to the office to teach a class, go to a meeting, or catch up on various administrative tasks. This quickly and easily added up to seventy hours a week. It had to stop.

Here's the blow to my ego. Though I had considered myself to be indispensable, I was amazed to find the parishioners at Anchor Park United Methodist Church did not. They were eager for me to get my life under control. I learned that my compulsion to work all the time came from my internal drive, not from their expectations. Their expectations were not at all unreasonable. I had just never taken the time to ask.

At a young age I had been placed in a position of responsibility that was beyond my experience. I was determined to succeed and I did, yet I was learning that the price I had paid was too high and that success could be achieved without surrendering to my own unreasonable expectations. While living like this fueled my ego, it did not address the congregation's need to create their own sense of commitment. Things like trustee meetings went along just fine without me. Why did I need to be there? I had no idea how to repair the boiler or negotiate with contractors over a new roof. The room was full of highly skilled professionals. On the morning of the first big snow of the season I woke up anxious. Oh no! We haven't contracted with anyone to plow the church parking lot. What a mess this will be! How could I have forgotten such a basic task? I dressed quickly, drove to the church and into a freshly plowed parking lot. Perhaps I wasn't indispensable after all.

As I learned to stay home, everyone's lives improved. Church leaders felt affirmed as I offered them a new level of trust. I began to keep reasonable office hours, to limit the number of meetings I would attend, and to teach fewer classes. I developed a renewed sense of intentionality in prayer, meditation, and study. In previous years, I had begun to experiment with keeping the Sabbath in a historically traditional manner. This practice had become inconsistent; I picked it up again with a healing vigor.

It's not easy for me to let go when the mind screams, "CONTROL!" That said, leaving in the middle of the day for a walk, devotional reading, and prayer is not wasted time. While I know this, I still had to remind myself over and over, this is important. It's not wasted time. I remembered Nouwen's admonition, "Without this wasted time, life becomes a series of incidents and accidents." When I had initially been offered this pastoral position, it was to provide spiritual direction and leadership. It was easy to lose this sense of focus when the ego says I must provide the answer to every question.

All of these practices contributed to my renewed commitment to live life to the full, or as my friend Rick had so joyfully announced before his own untimely death, "Live until you die!" Did I have a year, ten years, or sixty years? No one knows these things. What I did have was today, and if I lived today vigorously, faithfully, and with a commitment to love as deeply as possible, my life would come alive. The St. Louis Cardinal great, Stan Musial, was often teased by his teammates for his optimism. They would take bets on how many times he would say 'Wonderful' in a day. His life was so dominated by gratitude that wonderful was his default description. I became determined to live like that.

Ann and I had first come to Alaska out of a sense of faithfulness to our call as Christians. We came to offer ourselves as a pastoral family to a people and place not everyone could embrace. We had also come to honor our sense of adventure, and with a deep desire to grasp every opportunity life offered. We wanted to teach our children that a significant part of following God was to live a life that did not surrender to fear. With renewed intention, we began to explore, backpack, fish, hike, and travel. I continued to embrace adventure on a larger scale, climbing and skiing in the mountains, kayaking, and pushing the limits of my skill and endurance.

I believe that we reaped great dividends from renewing our commitment to this way of life. The church flourished, our children continued to develop their love of adventure, and Ann and I found a renewed sense of companionship. Even though the years provided a buffer from the trauma of coronary artery disease, always, somewhere in the back of my mind, a clock was ticking. Each occasional chest discomfort, shortness of breath, normal parts of life for everyone, caused me to wonder, *Is this my heart?*

More Life to Live

In 1999, when we arrived in Tucson, it had been eight years since my last cardiac event. I accepted a new pastoral assignment to St. Paul's United Methodist Church in Tucson, Arizona, and we moved. While I did not obsess on the idea of ten years, another episode requiring intervention was likely, and the thought was never far from my mind. As I quested for doctors, I didn't just make first appointments, I conducted full-fledged interviews. I knew that I must find people who cared about my values and the way I lived my life. The suggestion that some risk could be avoided by spending life passively on the couch was alien to me. I believed that my exercise, that many believed had become extreme, was one of the keys to my health. My quest for adventure brought me life. I could not imagine life without it. I found doctors who embraced this premise, and we developed close relationships as the years moved on. And it was years. I lived with careful attention from those doctors for another eight years.

I had now lived nearly twenty years since my last intervention. I couldn't help but wonder if I was one of a small number of people who mysteriously dodge the bullet. For unknown reasons some folks simply never develop symptoms again, no matter the length of time. Was I one of them?

In the spring of 2011, I registered for the Old Pueblo 50 Mile Endurance Run. This race, run through the Santa Rita Mountains of southern Arizona, is my neighborhood race. I had completed it seven times before. It is a difficult event and it was not getting easier as I got older. This year I chose to run because I was helping my colleague and friend Angie McCarty prepare for her first ultra, the Ouachita Trail 50 Mile Endurance Run Mile in Arkansas. An ultra is any race that is longer than the traditional marathon distance of 26.2 miles. Most ultras are run on trails which are much more challenging than running on roads. I wanted to be in superior shape at Ouachita so I could keep up and be an encouragement to her. My plan was to run Old Pueblo the first weekend in March and Ouachita, with Angie, six weeks later. I was in shape, feeling good, optimistic about the day. Ann and friends from our church managed an aid station for runners at mile twenty-nine. It generated a renewed sense of optimism to see them and to have a chance to grab my favorite mid-race snack, an ice-cold grape soda. At mile forty, Angie joined me as a pacer for the last ten miles. Around mile forty-five, I was debilitated by stomach distress and cramps. While some stomach distress is common for me in these events, this was far beyond that norm, and the cramps were brutal. My calf muscles knotted from the cramping, causing me to fall. As I was crossing a small, fast-running creek, my calf cramped again and I fell into the water. Angie had to help me up. Since she was a pacer, she was required to stay with me for the balance of the race. I knew a little mud and blood running down from my knees just added some drama to the story. Though the severity of these unexpected issues did cross my mind, I knew my running friends would laugh them off. The end of most ultras looks a bit like a M.A.S.H. unit with people curled up on the ground and others hovering ill around the edge of the crowd. This is physically stressful stuff. I dismissed my issues, and hoped for a better day at Ouachita. I spent a couple of weeks recovering, then ramped up my training for Ouachita without incident.

As we lined up for the starting gun at Ouachita, I fully expected this would be a good day. The weather was cool, partly cloudy, and this course was not as hard as Old Pueblo. Ann and Angie's family were cheering for her and this big event. They patted me on the back with the simple expectation.

I would be fine.

I have done this a lot.

It rates no-big-deal status among my family and friends. It's simply expected.

At mile seventeen Angie pulled ahead, disappearing from my sight as she rounded a corner and crested a hill. It was okay; in running events this long we rarely stay together the entire time. That is not our intention. We would run together later. I was winded and nauseous early. But by mile forty something else was clear to me: I was experiencing intermittent chest pain. I decided to be safe and walk in. While that stabbing feeling in the middle of my chest was no friend, it was familiar. I knew it by name. I knew it in my heart.

Ten miles was a long walk after a forty-mile run. Ten fearful, discouraged miles felt like an even longer walk. As I prepared to enter the finish area, Ann came down the road to greet me. She was worried. She had expected me to be much faster today. I was dead last, a new and humiliating experience for me. I was confident that I had not had a heart attack, yet I was also confident that the blockages in my left anterior descending artery had returned. Not wanting to dampen Angie's well-earned joy, I did not say anything then. Like the others, I was proud of her accomplishment. Besides that, it is difficult for people to take you seriously when you say you have heart problems at the finish line of a fifty-mile event, even when you are last. At that moment, it sounded like loser's limp.

While I wanted to go to my room and hide, the day wasn't done. It was my fifty-seventh birthday, so my friends surprised me at the hotel with a cake. Everyone was happy. I was happy for them and set my anxiety aside as I joined in the congratulatory storytelling and laughter. Angie, her husband, Sam, and all three of their kids were thrilled with their mother's success. As Ann cut my birthday cake and passed it around, the usual joking about age stung deeper than I had expected. A visiting friend cracked a joke, "The good thing about being over the hill is that there's nothing left to learn the hard way."

I thought to myself, *Shut up! You have no idea what you are talking about.*

Later that night, I told Ann what had happened. We held each other for a while. Having practiced this moment in our imaginations for the past decade, there didn't seem to be much to say. Unless I was mistaken, a bypass was in my near future. I had learned to listen to my body well; I was not mistaken. The next day I took a walk by myself, called my cardiologist, Mason Garcia, and made an appointment for my first day back in Tucson.

After a month of what seemed like endless diagnostic tests, Ann, my doctors, and I decided that I would have a minimally invasive cardiac bypass and graft. This is known as CABG, like the vegetable. Instead of the traditional entry through the sternum, they would make an incision below my left breast and crack two ribs as they found their way to my heart. There they would use my mammary artery to complete the bypass. If others were needed, they would harvest an artery from my leg, which they did. I lived in Tucson, but we took the two-hour drive to Scottsdale so that Dr. Michael Catsky could perform the surgery. When we met, he asked me why I chose him. "Because Dr. Garcia, my cardiologist, says that you are the best in the world."

He smiled and said matter of factly, "Dr. Garcia is right. I have a gift and almost every day I get to use it. Each day, twice on most days, I reach into someone's chest, lift up their heart, and save their life. I'm going to save yours."

I believed him, and we agreed that I would check in the hospital the next morning at seven to prepare for surgery. I was strangely excited. It felt like the night before an ultra for which I was well prepared. Years ago, I had promised myself that when this day came, I would be able to look in the mirror and say with assurance that I had done the best I could. It was a promise I had kept. That night, Ann, our sons, my friend Derek, and I went to Chase Stadium to watch the Arizona Diamondbacks and the Chicago Cubs play baseball. The great American pastime provided a welcome diversion.

The next morning, we arrived at the hospital a little early. I went to the counter to check in, and the nice woman smiled at me and said, "Mr. Still, your surgery has been canceled." My imagination went crazy. I am unfamiliar with panic. I'm great in a crisis. This time I was struggling not to fall apart. Perhaps they had decided I was a hopeless case and didn't want to waste their resources on me. Or had my insurance company refused to pay? I asked for an explanation, but she had none. It seemed odd to me that she would not know why. Fueled by distrust, I gently touched her elbow and said, "I am your constant companion until you find out why."

"You are serious, aren't you?"

"Yes, I am."

I followed her from desk to desk as she searched for information. Finally, she handed me the phone and said, "Your surgeon is on the phone. You ask him."

"Dr. Catsky, this is Billy Still."

"Yes," he said groggily.

"What's up? You are not here." This felt like a dumb thing to say. Surely, he knew he was not here.

"I was up all night saving someone else's life. I'm going to take a nap before I save yours. Some of my colleagues think it is heroic to operate all night and all day. I think it is arrogant. I'm going to take your heart in my hands. If I am not perfect, your life will be ruined. Take care of yourself today, and I'll take care of you tomorrow."

Ann, our sons, and various friends who had come to join us went to our hotel to hang out for the day. It was not much fun, but I was grateful for their presence. We returned to Chase Stadium that night. The home team lost to the Cubs once again. This provided another diversion, as well as an odd bit of encouragement. The Cubs, baseball's perennial, lovable losers, were winners tonight. I was feeling like a hopeful loser going into extra innings.

Recently, I reviewed an entry in my journal from this day. I had written, I have been working as hard as I can to maintain the practice of truth-telling without complaining—with mixed results. We learned the difference between the two in church a few weeks ago. When I complain, I am powerless. I blame others for things I can do nothing about. I become a victim in this quest to blame others and expect them to satisfy my concerns while I sit idly by.

I am in pain; why can't you people help me?

I take really good care of my body. Why do I have this disease?

These are dead-end questions that only lead to darkness. They drive people away, leaving me isolated and alone. When I tell the truth, I take my power back.

I hurt. What will I do about it? Can you help me? Perhaps it's okay to hurt.

I have a disease. There will be a life-saving intervention. What will I do with this fifth chance at life?

This is a road that leads to light. I am no longer a victim. There is no one to blame, no Why? Just a great big beautiful, what now? People are eager to join me on this journey, and I am no longer alone.

The next morning when we arrived at the hospital, Dr. Catsky was there. He assured me that he was well rested, fresh, and ready to play ball. I mercifully fell asleep under the influence of the anesthetic and did not wake until the surgery was over. I had been told that there would be an intubation tube in my throat when I woke. They told me this so I would not panic, as people sometimes do. They said the tube would help me breathe, that this was not unusual, but could be uncomfortable and irritating. When my breathing was normalized, it would be removed. As I emerged from the fog of anesthesia, I felt around and realized that there was no tube in my throat. I began to thrash about in a drug-induced panic. I could not speak. The nurse tried to calm me, asking what was wrong.

"The tube, where is the tube? Why don't I have a tube in my throat?"

While the nurse was trying to decipher the source of my panic, I wondered, *Maybe I'm dead and that is why. Maybe they think I'm dead. I don't think I am dead. I should let them know!*

I have no idea how long it took her to understand my concern, probably no more than seconds. Finally, she understood. She smiled and stroked my head with one hand while gently rubbing my arm with the other. "You don't have an intubation tube," she said. "In all my years of nursing, you are the first cardiac bypass surgery patient I have seen that didn't need help breathing. Your lungs are so strong, it's not necessary."

I fell back into a blissful and agonizingly painful sleep, thinking nurses are saints. After a five-day hospital stay, I returned home.

My friend Derek, who was always pushing me to the next level, asked me to reflect on a question I was still too tired to ask myself. What have I learned through this great adventure? I knew he was hoping for deep, insightful, existential truth. I gave him what I had. I told him that I felt like our small children, who wondered who would take care of them those long years ago when this journey began. I was not well enough for deep thoughts, so I thought about the sacred ordinary, the quotidian that is at once mundane and meaningful. If I was to find meaning in all of this, it had to be in the simplicity of the moment. I could think no further.

In the hospital, even without the intubation tube, I once had many tubes invading my body. I asked how many. I wrote it down. I wondered, *Why are there so many tubes here, and what happens when they are removed?* These are thoughts I had.

I heard someone say something about Monday. I thought, *It can't be Monday. I am confident it's Wednesday afternoon. It was Monday morning. Was I ahead or behind? What happened to those lost days?* These were my concerns.

The next morning I thought, *I don't know how to get out of bed. What if I can't get out of bed?* That kind of question.

Later that day, I thought, *There must be a less painful way to put on a shirt.* That kind of curiosity.

And then, the things I could not do at all.

The next day my bishop, mentor, and friend Bill Dew died. His wife, Mitzie, not realizing I had just had surgery, called from their home in Sacramento to tell me. Propped up with pillows and moving slowly, I was not sure I could pick up my cell before it quit ringing. I struggled and was able to do it. I only answered because I saw her name on the screen. We talked for a few moments as Mitzie described Bill's last moments. Then she asked me to speak at his memorial service. I had spoken at two of his retirement celebrations. I practiced deep breathing so that I could tell her no, and why, without crying. I lost that struggle. She and I cried on the phone together. I felt an overwhelming powerlessness and guilt, longing to do one more thing for my bishop and friend. It was not that I was complaining that he died. It was not unexpected. He would not complain, either. He was an eminently wise and practical man. He would have affirmed my telling the truth about deep grief and not being able to put on and take off one's shirt without help.

Many gathered to honor his life. I did this in the painful privacy of my home. Unable to travel, I honored my friend in solitude. I thought about the wound in my chest and the healing heart that lay beneath it.

My bishop told me once that every pastor had two or three topics to which they always returned. His primary topic was resurrection.

Was this new life, a step toward the end of life, or both? Was this a kind of resurrection?

He had helped me interpret many of life's major crises. Was his life theme one around which I might begin to rebuild my own life?

I felt bound, imprisoned, chained to the chair, and unable to think beyond, *How do I care for myself? What if I will always be this way?*

Recovery was long and slow; I was impatient. I was not supposed to drive the car for a month. One day, a few days before the deadline, I could not take it anymore. I got into my car, pulled out of the driveway, and headed to the movie theater. I was eager to get there on my own, sit alone, and watch a movie. I didn't care what it was. Halfway there, I realized Ann would get home before I would. I didn't want to cause her to worry, so I pulled into a parking lot and called her office.

"Hey, Billy, how are you?" she asked.

"Great. I just thought you would want to know I am going to the movie." A long pause then, "With whom?"

"Alone."

"How will you get there?"

"I'm driving. It's okay to be mad. I'm not calling to discuss it. I just had to leave. I will drive to the trailhead at the end of the road and take a walk in the desert after the movie is over. I'll be home after that."

"This feels like a very poor choice," she said, not trying to mask her deep frustration.

"Yes," I agree. "It does feel like a poor choice, but it's what I am going to do. I'll see you later," I said, working hard to sound matter of fact so that we would not have to discuss this further.

After the movie, I drove to the Trailhead. It was about eight and dark. I am comfortable in the desert at night and have an intimate knowledge of these trails. Besides, I wouldn't be going far. It would just be a slow, hot, dusty shuffle. I put my headlamp on and began to trudge the seven-tenths of a mile to a picnic table, a long rest, then the walk back. The desert is alive at night, and so it was no surprise to see a Western diamondback rattler curled up in the trail. I knew we were no threat to each other. For a few moments I looked at this beautiful creature, then walked on by. The snake did not acknowledge me in any way. Danger, potential death, lurking around the corners of our lives, is not always dramatic; it's just there.

My life became a constant tug between the wisdom of taking it easy and pushing myself. Stay on the couch too long, and your body and spirit atrophies. Get up too vigorously or too soon, and you will be driven back to the couch, or worse. I wanted to run. I had to run. Two months post-surgery, I tried to run for the first time.

Ann walked with me out the front door where we were met by Angie, and a couple of other friends, Tommy and Mark. They were there to encourage us on this momentous day. We all ran and walked three miles on streets in my neighborhood. Although no one was willing to say it, they were nervous and did not want to be too far from a car in case something went wrong. At one point, while I was running, I looked and saw that they were all walking and keeping up. I told them that they must at least look like they are running, or I would become discouraged and quit. They began to laugh and bounce up and down.

For me, it was painful and painfully slow.

The first time I rode my bicycle post-surgery, I rode alone. Everyone was afraid I would fall and hurt myself. I was afraid too and did not want to ride with the burden of their fear and mine; I slipped away on my own. I was so slow that, as I climbed a small hill, I thought the crosswinds might push me over. However, time really does heal many things, even hearts, and I was confident, correctly, that the next time would be better and the next time better than that. After a while this rapid improvement would plateau into a slower rate of progress.

On the first anniversary of my heart surgery, I woke to find myself unexpectedly emotional. I rolled over, threw my leg over Ann's, pulled her shoulder tight against mine, and, as if that wasn't enough, began to poke her a bit in a joking way that I appreciate and she does not.

"Hey," I said. "Good morning. Did you know that today is the anniversary of my surgery?"

"Yes," she said. "That's nice. It's all working out, isn't it?" Then she moved my legs, straightened the quilt, and rolled back over.

I went to work and walked into Angie's office. "Hey," I said, "Today is the anniversary of my surgery."

With casual interest, she said, "Yeah, isn't that great?" Then, without lifting her fingers from the keyboard, she said, "Could you get your sermon material to me by noon?"

On this morning I wanted the world and everyone in it to stop and pay attention to me. The world had its own agenda.

It became clear that this anniversary was not a big deal to anyone else. If I was to avoid walking around all day with my feelings hurt, I was going to have to do something to mark it. On my own. Alone. Writing letters was the answer. Doctors Selmon, Beacham, Pazzi, Garcia, and Catsky saved my life. I decided that I would write each of them a personal letter of gratitude, assuring them that I realized I had been given multiple chances for a new life and that I did not intend to squander them. I wanted to tell them that the way they used their gifts mattered, that I noticed and was grateful. I wanted to help them take a step on their pathway to peace, just as they had helped me stay on mine. I wanted them to be confident; it was my intent to live until I die.

There is never a time when we are completely sheltered from those things that would cause us to lose our center, robbing us of our journey on the pathway to peace. There is never a time when we are completely sheltered from the extravagant, compassionate, merciful love of God.

147

There never has to be a time when we are sheltered from the love of our faith communities and faithful friends. So today, let the crosswinds blow, we will not be knocked over. We will love and be loved, mourn and cry, tell stories and laugh. We will treat every day as a gift that marks the entrance into a new era. We will ride and not be weary; we will run and not faint. We will courageously and with patience follow the markers that lead us on the pathway to peace.

Even with the Sounds of Gunfire

Hosea and I sat side by side on a log in the village of John Dean Town, Liberia, isolated from the hundreds of people who surrounded us. This was to be a goodbye.

On that day the sky, often cloudy in this tropical rain forest, was bright with sunlight, causing me to squint as I looked at my friend Hosea. This man, who had experienced more violence than I had imagined existing in the world, had become a bright light to me. He embraced a grace so vibrant and deep that my very soul squinted as I tried to look inside his. In an awkward attempt to say thank you, I reached into my daypack and took out a pair of blue flip-flops I had purchased from a street vendor in Monrovia. Removing my shoes and socks, I slipped these on my feet. It was my intention to return home with as little as possible. This was not a significant sacrifice. Hosea had been like a bodyguard and had become my friend and mentor in the faith. I asked him if he would like my shoes. Looking down for a moment, I noticed my dirty socks lying on the log between us. He saw them too. Do I also offer my friend socks, stained with the sand from the forest trails and sweat from days of unwashed wear? He nodded in their direction as we caught each other looking at them. I picked them up and stuffed them into the shoes. I stretched out my hand toward him, a sock-stuffed shoe held in place between each thumb and index finger.

"What will you wear when you get home?" he asked.

"I have other shoes."

"How many pairs of shoes do you have?"

He sat beside me with feet that had rarely worn shoes. His calluses were thicker than my new flip-flops. I hoped that he was pleased and not insulted. I was not sure if he wanted my shoes to protect his feet or for the prestige of owning western shoes. How many pairs of shoes do I own? How many pairs of shoes do the poorest Americans own? How many do the privileged, like me, own?

This was my goodbye gift. Following a two-week visit with our friends in this remote West African village, our group from St. Paul's United Methodist Church, in Tucson, Arizona were headed back to the capital of Monrovia, and then on to Tucson. It was 2009, and the seventeen-year long war was over. What I had learned was that this unwinnable war had not been a war of ideology. It was anarchy. It consisted of senseless torture and slaughter; no one had a clear explanation of why.

Our congregation has had a long-standing relationship with these folks who were trying desperately to move beyond the suffering of this civil war.

In this village, we had first supported local folks in building and staffing a school. While I had thought a medical clinic should come first, they had insisted a school was the priority. When I asked why a school before a medical clinic, they responded, "How will our children participate in rebuilding our country if they cannot read, write, and understand basic math?" They set the priorities. It was their village.

Faced with the opportunity to turn around and learn, I ask myself, Why do I think I know what's best for these folks? They live here. They lived through the war. I must quiet my will, and honor their voices.

In the early 2000s, people in Liberia believed that they were nearing the end of the war and the future at last loomed brightly on the horizon. At that time, we sent money to purchase building supplies for the school. When the supplies were first purchased in Monrovia and delivered to the village, great excitement rose among the local people. A messenger was sent the full day's journey from the village to the town of Buchanan, hoping for access to a phone or email. They wanted to tell us: they had received the supplies and begun the work. They were so eager for us, their as-yet unmet American friends, to receive this good news. They contacted their bishop, who contacted me. Worlds apart, every contact deepened our commitment to live in relationship with our Liberian friends.

Local people began the labor and where there was paid work, they received the jobs. They were quite competent and did not need us to come and do the work for them. One day, while folks were working, they heard the horrifying sounds of trampling feet and gunfire. Rebels emerged from the forest, threatening the edge of the clearing. The villagers had no weapons and no desire to fight, so they gathered their children and fled. The rebels did not bother to pursue them. Instead they took the building supplies: lumber, tools to mix mortar, and bricks, and the few hammers, saws, shovels, and axes. The work ceased.

Our friends did not want to tell us about this. They were afraid that we would lose confidence in them and their ability to manage this project. Some thought we would decide they were a bad investment and that we would not want to help them if they could not protect themselves.

John Innis, the bishop of the United Methodist Church in Liberia shared this sad information with me on the back porch of my home in Tucson, Arizona. A world away from Liberia, Bishop Innis had come to tell our congregation. As he told the story, we sat drinking tea and eating sandwiches. Warm, safe, and well fed, the thought of troops at the edge of my clearing was beyond my imagining, and though I understood their way of thinking, it broke my heart to know they harbored this fear and shame. When I shared this news with our Tucson church, our commitment to investing in their future increased. We had been working with this group for a few years; we couldn't imagine turning away.

Our congregation helped them replace the stolen building supplies so that by the time of my first visit to Liberia, in 2005, the school had been in operation for three years. After that, a hand-pumped and filtered water well was installed. This might seem like a small thing, but it was huge. The year before, 138 children in this area died of diarrhea, cholera, and other dirty water diseases. Imagine going to a small town of 5,000 residents and snatching away 138 children. Imagine burying your children one at a time, day after day. Even in a place as devastated by war as Liberia, this pain was unthinkable.

The year after we installed the pump, the number of child deaths by water-borne illness became eight. One hundred and thirty children's lives saved annually for an initial investment of twenty-five hundred dollars and an additional one hundred dollars a year for maintenance. When I stood before the church in Tucson and asked, we raised the money in a few minutes. Twenty-five hundred dollars is not a significant sacrifice to a group of Americans. For a teacher in the school in John Dean Town, it represents two and a half years' salary.

By the time I made my first trip to Liberia, in February of 2005, the war was mostly over. The UN appointed an interim government. The cruel despot, Charles Taylor, was being tried for war crimes. Still, the circumstances were not easy. When my friend Will Miles and I arrived at the Monrovia International Airport, we were on the one flight from

Europe that arrived each week. Will and I immediately found ourselves moving as a pair of oddly privileged Americans through the airport in a seemingly endless sea of chaotic humanity. Luggage was piled in the middle of a large room, and it was left to each person to dig through it and find your own. After that, we were funneled outside into what appeared to be field after field of people and abandoned vehicles. There was a single small terminal. Across the street stood the remnant of the airport that before the war had been modern and beautiful. In places where the walls once stood, African Union peacekeepers sat. Many were barefoot and shirtless. They were propped up behind sandbags, machine guns in hand.

We expected to be met at the airport by representatives of the bishop's office. We were surprised that no one greeted us or offered a ride into town. No one even told us where the town was. It was stiflingly hot, and the only place to purchase food or water was from the children, who wandered through the crowd, carrying plastic bags of each on their heads. We were pretty sure that we did not want to eat or drink from these vendors until we found someone who could help us determine what was safe and what was not. At this point, we did not know anyone.

None of this sound's unusual to folks who travel through the war-torn countries of West Africa, but at that time it was foreign to Will and me. While I'm not sure who deserves original credit for this quote, we laughed, wiped the dusty sweat from our faces and recalled the travelers' motto, "In the end, everything will be alright. If everything is not alright, it must not be the end."

Trusting that the end would be okay, we hitched a ride into town and located the bishop's compound where we would stay for the next week. The compound consisted of several small houses, the bishop's larger home, guest rooms, and a work-shed, all surrounded by concrete walls about twelve feet high. This felt familiar to Will. Much of his childhood was spent in post-WWII Germany. He was familiar with walls topped by broken bottles, jagged edges turned up, cemented into the top of concrete walls that surround houses. Once there, we were informed that the bishop was in Ivory Coast. No one was sure exactly when he would return.

We realized we were on an adventure. This pleased both of us.

We set about meeting and learning about the people in and around the compound. The people we met in Monrovia seemed eager to find a sense of normalcy after roughly two decades of war. Groups of children in school uniforms walked back and forth each day. As I remember struggling to get my kids to do their homework, I was amazed by the passion for learning demonstrated by these children. Not allowed in the various compounds that lined the street, the children stayed out at night and huddled against the outside of those walls so that they could do their school work by the ambient light that filtered across. In a city with no electricity, light was produced by a couple of hours of generator power a day. Will remembered the strain of reading by generator.

Our first new friend is Malachi. He is a young Liberian man who does odd jobs around the compound. His current task is to take care of Will and me. Like every Liberian I meet, his voice is soft, lilting, and gentle. He wears old khaki pants, a floral shirt, and rubber flip-flops.

His clothes are worn, sparkling clean, and sharply pressed. He appears to be in his early twenties. Because of his youth, he has no memories that are not war experiences. It takes little more than hello to find that he is eager to tell his story. We spend the next couple of hours together, becoming friends, listening to his story, sitting in plastic chairs under a palm tree.

He begins by speaking of this mother. She is from Ghana. She cannot hide this because of the traditional tattoos on her face. Malachi tells me that one time Charles Taylor gathered all the foreigners who lived in the city of Buchanan together in one place, about four thousand of them. Rebel troops surrounded them and began shooting into the crowd and then into the piles of bodies. During the execution, they decided that they would let 163 live so that they could gather and prepare food for the soldiers. When asked, he has no idea how they arrived at the number, 163, but when people tell this story the number is cited with authority. Malachi was eleven on the day of the massacre. He and a friend stood weeping among a pile of dead bodies when a soldier in an officer's uniform thrust the barrel of a pistol against his forehead.

"Why are you crying?" he demanded to know.

"Because we hear the guns and we know that we are going to die."

"Who is your grandmother?" the officer asked. "Is she alive?"

Malachi wondered why this was important. He said that he asked himself if he would be executed because of his family ties. Did the officer know his grandmother? Would he die if he lied? He had no idea and his terrified eleven-year-old mind couldn't calculate the cost of his answer, so he simply told the truth. He offered her name, and then said, "She is still alive in her village."

"Then I will not kill you. Your grandmother paid my school fees when I was a child. Now, why are you crying?"

"Because we hear the sounds of gunfire."

"Stop crying and be grateful. As long as you hear the sounds of guns, you are alive." Then he turned to a group of troops behind him and ordered them to "let these dry-eyed boys pass and do not kill them".

Malachi told me at that moment he learned that God is alive even in the sounds of gunfire. He also told me that since he wiped his face that day, he has never shed another tear. His sadness runs too deep for tears. I have no idea what to say, so we embrace. He eases the tension with a smile and offers us tea. As I listened to this, I could not shake the awareness that all through their civil war Liberians believed that America would come to their rescue.

Our history and theirs are irrevocably intertwined. In the years before and after the American Civil War, a group of Americans decided they would repatriate slaves to Africa. They did not consider that by then most slaves had never been to Africa and that the ones who had been came from many different places. The US Marines took the harbor that is now Monrovia and deposited shiploads of people there. The indigenous people were violently relocated. Although this is not the source of the current war in Liberia, descendants of former American slaves, known as Americos, and the indigenous people of the area, are still in conflict. American history is alive in street names as well as the names of cities. The capital is Monrovia, named after the US President James Monroe. The next largest city is Buchanan.

As Will and I, accompanied by Malachi, walk through the endless shanty towns that flow from the edges of Monrovia, people approach us and in a conspiratorial tone they ask, "Are you a friend of Bill Clinton?" It's 2005, but they are unaware that George Bush has been president for four years. Bill Clinton is universally admired because he once sent two hundred marines into Monrovia to protect the US Embassy. Liberians thought it was the beginning of America coming to the rescue. They were wrong.

Next they ask, "Are you CIA?" I ask Malachi for the proper response. It may matter. As we wander the streets of Monrovia together, Will and I are the only European faces we see. Malachi says that if I am a friend of Bill Clinton, it will be good for his prestige. Not so good if I am CIA. So for the rest of our time in Monrovia, we walk the street serenaded by the familiar refrain, "Are you a friend of Bill Clinton?"

"Yes."

"Are you CIA?"

"No."

"Are you sure you are not CIA?"

"I'm sure."

Immediately after this exchange, men hold us in an embrace. Small children touch our skin, then run away crying and laughing. Malachi says that they think we have a skin disease since we are so white, pasty, and soaked with sweat. He wonders the same thing. I acknowledge that most of the people in the world are brown and tell him that many people in the US sit in the sun hoping our white skin will darken. Malachi nods his head in understanding. "Dark skin is more beautiful," he agrees.

Women watch from a distance. While women in Liberian culture are quite powerful and social in conversation, they do not approach us on the streets as men do. Any public show of affection between men and women would be culturally inappropriate.

As Malachi, Will, and I wander through a street market in Monrovia I ask, "Malachi, what happened to all the rebel troops? Where are they now?" Looking around I realize that there are hundreds, perhaps thousands of young men wandering the streets.

With dawning insight, I ask, "How many of these young men were rebel troops?"

"All of them," he replies. "All but one," and he lowers his head and places the palm of his hand over his heart. I realize that for now, it's time to stop the questions, but there is one more that cannot be silenced.

"How do you make peace with the idea that one of these men may have gunned down your family that day in Buchanan?"

"I do not think of them individually. It is not the crime of any one man. I simply know that it must stop, so I repent of the ugliness in my heart and offer them grace. I pray that they will offer me grace also. In time, the obligation of love will require us to live in peace."

I hear this refrain over and over, and it is so far beyond my life experience that I am never sure how to respond. Every Liberian we meet treats it as a mantra of the heart. "The violence must stop. Peace must begin with me. In time, the obligation of love will require us all to live in peace."

I am in awe of this community decision to embrace redemption.

It is such an unreasonable choice. It is the only reasonable choice.

So I walk, listen, and look at these young men, trying not to guess, rebel troop or not?

The next day I am traveling with my friend Naomi, who is a United Methodist pastor and Liberian. Liberians have no problem with women in leadership and will soon elect the first African female head of state, Ellen Johnson Sirleaf. Naomi is taking us to see some small Liberian churches. The bishop has loaned us his driver and his jeep for today's adventure. As we move about Liberia, I have noticed that Liberian women dress beautifully. I am embarrassed by my poor dress in their company. Until I begin to receive African shirts as gifts, I was usually dressed in shorts and a t-shirt. Women here are elegantly dressed, and not just on special occasions. Walking the city streets, going about daily business, carrying on with chores in the villages, women wear brightly colored material wrapped around as a dress and matching headscarves. Farther from town, in rural villages, women often work topless with the beautiful material tied at the waist. They use a white, pasty substance to paint decorative patterns on their chest and neck. When we arrive, they immediately place a wrap around their chest. We stop by Naomi's house for a short break. The group we are with step outside, so Naomi and I sit in her living room alone. I ask her about the bright colors, the beautiful dress, and while I suspect they are part of a long cultural tradition, she provides heartbreaking insight from the war.

"We do not know if we will be beautiful tomorrow. I do not know how to tell you what it is like to see your closet emptied and all of your dresses thrown onto a fire in front of your house. Then you are forced to lie, stripped naked, on the floor, with soldiers standing over you, mocking you, spitting on you, trying to decide if they have time to rape you, and if they do, if everyone can take you or just the officers. They take everything of beauty from your heart and your home. Today I want to be beautiful because I can. All Liberian women want to be beautiful, so we take our colorful clothing and wrap it around our bodies. It masks the scars of our broken hearts. We appear to be more beautiful than the men because we are."

I do not ask any questions about what may have happened on the day she mentioned. Was it one day? Did this happen often? Was she taken by all the troops? She has a stunningly beautiful glow to her face, and I do ask her about that. How, I want to know, can she appear so lovely, joyful, and filled with gladness after so much evil? She smiles, says nothing, and squeezes my hand as she adds another chapter to the mantra of Liberians offering grace to create a future with hope. Listening to her, watching her face as she speaks, I am overwhelmed by the context of her life. Immersed in memories of horror, she chooses to embrace the beauty of the moment. She is strong, powerful, and beautiful, and she knows it. No one can take this from her.

Each day, I hear these stories. I wonder, *What do I have to offer these people beside money and the things it can buy?* These are important, and in the world where I live, there is plenty of it. But what unites both of our worlds is a startling longing for grace. They are teaching me to receive it. Like Naomi, I want to be beautiful today. Her complexion is flawless, her clothing perfect. As she speaks, her eyes dance with delight, then quickly flow with rivers of tears. The tears are momentary as she moves with seeming ease back into the moment. Her beauty radiates love.

I realize how easily I neglect the practice of the most basic admonition to love.

In a biblical passage, the apostle Paul writes, "If I give away all of my possessions, and if I give over my body so that I may boast, but do not have love, I gain nothing. Love is patient; love is kind; love is not envious or boastful or arrogant or rude. It does not insist upon its own way; it is not irritable or resentful." As I listen to Paul, I think he is asking too much. I know he has been to prison before he wrote this, but how does he believe that he can just order people to love this fully? Then I realize that it is not an order; it is a statement of possibility. In time, through the grace of God, without regard to our circumstance, this is who we can decide to become. "Love does not rejoice in wrongdoing, but rejoices in the truth. It bears all things, believes all things, hopes all things, endures all things. Love never ends." Paul, another person inexplicably jailed and tortured by his government, embraces fully a love that merely tugs at the borders of my heart.

This is a grace too deep for me to understand.

On this first trip in 2005, I am in Liberia for two reasons. Will and I have been invited to make first-hand acquaintances with church leaders and our friends in John Dean Town. And I am the ordination preacher at the Liberian Annual Conference of the United Methodist Church. Preaching at ordination creates quite a bit of anxiety for me. I preach a lot; preaching is not the issue. But these folks? What have I to say to them? These folks have endured Jesus-on-the-cross-type suffering for decades. Every one of them has stories that chill to the bone.

Me? I'm a well-educated, affluent, white man from Arizona with health insurance, a pension plan, two cars, a nice house, and countless pairs of shoes. After I preach, people will be ordained as deacons, deaconesses, and elders. Ninety-seven deacons, seventy-five deaconesses, and fifty elders. How did these folks meet the denominational requirements of ordination in the chaos that is their lives? How do they arrive here, filled with the confidence of hope? My heart turns to the author of the biblical book of Hebrews who, when speaking of the great heroes and heroines of faith says, "Yet all these, though they were commended for their faith, did not receive what was promised, since God had provided something better so that they would not, apart from us, be made perfect."

If God has something better for these folks, now is the time to give it to them. They have suffered enough.

I am sitting in the front of the church considering these things. As I wait to present the ordination sermon, hymns rise from the congregation like waves crashing on the shore. Chills run up and down my spine. On the dais are bishops, leaders of the Liberian church, and me. It is so hot that sweat soaks through my shirt, my liturgical robe, and the stole that adorns it. We are dwarfed by a long, winding old-English-style pulpit that curves its way out over the congregation. A sanctuary that would seat five hundred in my hometown of Tucson seats one thousand here with others looking in windows and crowding doorways.

It is time for me to preach. As I begin to stand, I hear the disruption of trucks pulling up on the street outside. The bishop takes my arm and tells me to wait. "Don't worry," he says. "It's all a show."

Troops surround the church. Men in suits barge in, walk up and down the aisle inspecting the crowd, speaking into their lapels. The crowd murmurs, "Friends of Bill Clinton? CIA?" I have no idea. With unchallenged authority, they clear the front row to respectful, yet muted, applause. His Excellency, Chairman of the United Nations-appointed interim Government of Liberia, John Bryant, enters and takes his seat.

I offer silent prayers of repentance as I once more walk up the long steps to the pulpit, lean out over the crowd and appeal for grace. A sea of eager faces meets mine. I stop and make eye contact with as many as I can, and then I begin to read from the book of Ezra. The prophet describes a scene as exiled Israelites return to Jerusalem and begin to rebuild the temple.

"Old people who had seen the first temple on its foundation wept with a loud voice when they saw this house, though many shouted aloud for joy, so that the people could not distinguish the sound of the joyful shout from the sound of the people's weeping."

After the sermon, our bishop invites His Excellency to the front of the church. I find out later that they have known each other since childhood. The bishop orders Bryant to kneel while he lays hands on him and prays. He asks me and a few others to join him in the laying on of hands. While I am confident that God hears this prayer, I am just as confident that John

Bryant was being prayed at as seriously as he was being prayed for. For thirty minutes or more the bishop roared his admonition to God and Mr. Bryant. The crowd shook the building to its foundation as they announced their approval with thunderous stomping and loud cries to God.

When we return to our seats, the bishop leans toward me and asks, "Was that okay?"

His question surprises me. "I thought I was the only one who was unsure of himself," I reply.

"You were unsure of yourself?" he asks.

As we move through the ordination liturgy, I move through the crowd of ordinands offering each one the gift of a Bible from boxes of old Bibles sent from somewhere in the United States. All of them are well worn, and no two are alike. This is the book that is to provide the foundation of their teaching and their lives. The war they have survived and their hopes for the future provide the context for reading its stories. As we approach the end of the affirmations of faith and prayers, it becomes clear that we will run out of Bibles. I walk back to my seat and get mine, and then I take the bishops' Bibles, and the Bibles from a few others sitting in the front.

I am carried away with the moment, I do not think to ask. I just take them and give them to these women and men kneeling on the hard, hot, tile floor, filled with vision, overflowing with grace, far more courageous than I. I imagine them holding these sweat-stained, cherished books in the front of village churches all over Liberia. The Americans who sent them here considered them used up. They were so wrong. These torn covers are coming to life, perhaps for the first time. Then, for one light-hearted moment, I imagine the bishops going back to their seats and looking for their Bibles!

In 2009, four years after that momentous ordination service, I am back in Liberia, this time with a doctor and nurses for the opening of the medical clinic in John Dean Town. The bishop and our crew from Tucson drive from Monrovia to Buchanan, about five hours on a dirt road that has had no maintenance in almost twenty years.

On the way, we pass through the Firestone Rubber Plantation. The rough bouncing in the back of our jeep eases off, and I look out the window. How beautiful the plantation is. I am momentarily grateful that it boasts a paved road, the only one I have seen in Liberia. On one million lush, green, well-manicured acres, leased for one hundred years at six cents an acre; this plantation provides rubber for tires all over the world. During the war, Liberian people saw that the rubber plantations continued to operate, diamond mines remained active, timber was harvested, and all of this by companies from the United States and the European Union. These were exempt from the destruction. Now the Chinese have entered the picture. No tires are produced in Liberia; the rubber is taken out of the country. The jobs that produce the tires and the tires themselves are of no benefit to local people. So the workers live in thatched huts with dirt floors, just like other rural Liberians.

I ask myself if I have Firestone tires on my car. I do not know. I have what was on sale when I bought new tires. Am I complicit in this complicated removal of assets? It is so easy to blame others and leave myself out of the equation.

Perhaps life on the rubber plantation is a little gentler. As far as I know, the immediate ravages of war spared their villages. Maybe there was a medical clinic and an elementary school. At the same time, it is clear these folks do not receive the benefits afforded by the rubber they spend their lives harvesting.

I didn't do any of this, did I? While our government twice invaded Iraq, I wasn't even aware of the suffering of the people of Liberia, and now I find myself received with extraordinary grace and confidence that I can be trusted. Wallowing in guilt is not helpful, but perhaps, as I learn to think differently, I can allow myself to choose new ways of living. I begin to wonder what they might be. Such grace must require vigorous turning on my part.

As I pray in the context of the Liberian villagers, I offer my heart and life for a change of direction while acknowledging that I have little idea what that means. Can I change the world? Can our congregation do that? Maybe not, but we can have a measurable impact on one little spot called John Dean Town, and they on us. That is why we are here.

The journey continues. Next, we take a series of increasingly deteriorating dirt roads and jeep trails for another several hours. By now, we eagerly anticipate the end of the road. I have been here before and tell my companions to be prepared for a warm greeting. But even I am shocked when we arrive. Hundreds of people greet us, jumping up and down and singing, "Welcome, you are welcome! We did not believe you would come. Welcome, you are welcome!" We are offered oranges and bottled water as our luggage disappears into the crowd, along with assurances that it will reappear later. People give us chickens with their legs tied together for easy transport. Others arrive with goats on the end of a rope.

Children reach out to hold our hands as we begin the ten-kilometer walk through the forest, laughing, dancing, and singing the entire way. These children are not afraid of us like the children in Monrovia were. When we arrive in John Dean Town, we find thatch huts, dirt floors, common cooking areas in the middle of the various small villages, and masses of happy children everywhere. I realize that this sounds somewhat like an idyllic scene from a movie about Albert Schweitzer, but this is what it was like. This village was much cleaner and more joyful than the city. Even so, this joy masks the same memories of wartime terror that they share with their urban friends.

I make a friend named Jonah. We sit on a small brick wall and watch the folks moving around in the open field in the center of the village. Men and women offer no displays of public affection to each other, but men do hold hands with men as they walk, and women with women. Children run around as they like, and I never see anyone scold them.

Jonah and I sit side by side. I ask, "Who is your wife?"

He points to a woman and says, "That is my wife." Then he points to another and says, "And that is my wife." He continues to scan the crowd as he says, "My other wife is not here." I ask how many wives he has. He tells me three, and then is surprised to learn that I have only one. "Is that enough?" he asks. I assure him that it is.

He laughs and says, "Well, three is expensive." As I make new friends, I remind myself that I am not being invited to evaluate their lives. His marriages are the result of cultural patterns that predate recorded history. Along with others, he offers grace to rebels who have tortured people in his village. What do I know of grace? Over time, we learn about each other, the fabric of our living, and find ourselves wrapped in mutual respect and love.

Jonah pulls out a day planner someone has given him. It seems an odd gift. We have learned that when people arrive at the medical clinic and we ask intake questions that would be normal in an American setting, no one here can answer questions about their age or when they were born. These are bright, eager people invested in their future, but questions about time just don't matter to them. So Jonah is curious, and asks about all the holidays in his day planner. I struggle to explain Boxing Day. There are no Canadians around to help. He asks about Mother's Day and Father's Day, telling me that for Liberians Mother's Day is a big event, Father's Day, not so much. We laugh and I say it is the same in America.

After a while I rise from the fallen tree. I join the children who walk across a football-sized field to the well. They carry back five-gallon buckets of water balanced on their heads. With an arrogance I fail to recognize, I think, if a small child can do this, so can I. I take a bucket, fill it with water, and place it on my head. A large crowd of children gather around me, laughing as I stagger back up the hill. There is a small, sharp, pointed piece of plastic on the bottom of the bucket. By the time I get the water to the cook station, it has pierced my scalp and blood is trickling down my face. The kids cannot wait for me to set it down, so they can show me that they wrap a towel under the bucket and on their head before they pick it up.

I cannot explain how at home I simply turn on the faucet, and clean water flows until I turn it off again. Several small children, recognizing my helplessness with such simple tasks, take me on as their project. They teach me how to care for myself and are always close at hand to help. They worry about me at night and wait around outside my room until they think I am safely asleep.

I am surprised to find that we have our own cooks. Sarah, a young woman in our group, makes a special effort to befriend the cooks. In a moment of bravery, she joins our hosts as they butcher a goat. They lead it away from the cooking area, and a young boy slits its throat and then its belly. He sticks his hands into the newly opened belly and pulls out the intestines. It is the first time she has smelled the warm blood of new death.

His hands stretch deeper inside the young, freshly killed goat. Its heart is still pumping blood. By that evening, its flesh is in our bowls, along with rice and greens. A few days later, Sarah joins the cooks as they prepare to kill a chicken. Everyone is impressed when she takes the chicken in her hands, grabs a machete, and beheads it herself.

I notice I have gained an unexpected companion: Hosea. He is an unusually muscular man with a gentle face, shaved head, and a strong sense of authority. Everywhere I go, he goes too. When I ask him about this, he says, "Liberia is a dangerous place. The bishop said if anything happens to you, it will be very bad for me, so I follow you everywhere. The Bishop told me to pay attention, that you are the kind of man who is eager to wander off and get lost. So if you wander off, it's okay, but I am coming with you."

For two weeks I rarely take a step without him. He is an amicable companion and an intimidating physical presence. His voice is Liberian, soft and gentle. When he speaks, he ends each sentence with an inquiring tone. It is as if he is hoping for a response. One day the conversation turns to the war. In Liberia every conversation eventually turns to the war.

I ask him, "What was it like for you in the war?"

He responds, "Oh, it was very hard. The rebels destroyed my home in Buchanan, so my family came out here to the forest. Of course the rebels were here too. For two years, I took charge of a group of about twenty-five people. Some died, some new ones came, some left, but most of the time it was twenty-five. We did not live in a village; we lived in the forest. We never stayed in the same place for two nights. We could not be found. After a short time, our clothes rotted off and we lived naked. It was as if we were animals. I would sneak into the edge of abandoned villages after dark to find food growing wild in untended gardens. We boiled water from the sea and scraped salt off the side of the dish. This made some people sick. Occasionally someone would be seen by a rebel on the trail. This rebel would search you to see if you had anything in a package, a tea bag, or packet of sugar. If you did, he would know you had been with people from a town, and he would not want them to know about him so he would kill you. If you did not have anything, he would want to sell you tea, salt, or sugar. You, of course, had no money, so he would ask, 'Shall I rape your women or just kill them?' There was nothing you could do. We moved every night, rarely building a shelter. One day, we realized that we had not seen rebels in a while. One by one, we came out of the forest, searching for family who would take us in. They thought of us as savages, but we were alive."

Later, after the war, one of the rebels who had burned Hosea's house showed up at his church. They recognized each other. This rebel offered him money to pay him for his house and to buy his silence, so he would not tell anyone what the rebel had done. Hosea said no. Reconciliation is not to be bought; reconciliation comes from the heart and over time.

I asked Hosea how could this be. How could he offer forgiveness and even more, reconciliation, to one who had done such evil? He looked at me with kind eyes and asked, "Billy, are you not a follower of Jesus Christ? The one who said love your enemies, bless those who persecute you, do not repay evil for evil?"

I thought of Naomi as I said that I was a follower of Jesus, and assured Hosea that Jesus had never asked me for this much. Hosea said, "If he did, you would give it, would you not?" I considered the small betrayals I had experienced in life and how deeply I held on to them. I looked up and in my imagination saw rebel troops racing across the village green, bullets flying, and people running in terror. I want someone to teach me about grace this deep. I turn to my friend and wait for him to speak.

"We forgive rebels and incorporate them into our community, so that we can be free and live peacefully. A grace this deep is always about us." As he said, "So we can be free," he spread his arms out to the village.

Even though I had heard similar things from many people during my first visit to Liberia, I began to wonder if going this far was the thinking of one extraordinary man, or if it remained a commonly held commitment among the people in the church. The village had a large green field surrounded on one side by the school, on another the medical clinic, and on another a gathering of huts where people lived and cooked. I decided to find my friend Jonah and ask him how he kept from thinking about revenge and retaliation. A very social fellow, he was not hard to find. I asked him to join me as we once again sat on a short brick wall, watched the children run around, and we spoke of things commonplace to him, deep beyond imagination to me.

He told me, "We are creating a community that expects people to forgive and move beyond forgiveness to the grace of reconciliation. In 2010 the UN Peacekeeping troops will leave, and we are anxious about that. We are afraid of what might happen, that the rebels will go back to the forest and dig up the weapons they have hidden there. So we teach people that we must live peacefully. This is very hard. We cannot do it alone, so we ask God to change our hearts. Since the beginning of time, these things have been true."

As I move from person to person, from experience to experience, it becomes clear to me that the repentance that leads to grace is also an act of profound and complex self-interest. I was not alone in this growing recognition of the primacy of grace. A remarkable turning began to occur.

Due to the constant witnessing of such deep grace by our Liberian friends, people from our Tucson group began to come to me, their pastor, to make their confession. Others spoke of resentments that had not served them well. Of how they had damaged their lives, marriages, and work environments. They were witnessing extraordinary acts of grace practiced in this war-torn place, largely abandoned by the world, and they (and I) wanted to learn this way of living.

The people here were teaching us. Not eager to belittle that pain, yet standing in the face of a nation where everyone held similar pain in countless multiples of agony, my Tucson friends announced their decision to search for gratitude and to learn to live a life dominated by this sense of goodness. We were learning to practice true repentance, the reorientation of one's life by turning and living in another direction.

Each day while in the village, in Liberia, I encounter folks who have fully embraced this repentance that leads them to offer grace on the deepest level. I join them in speaking of the longing of my heart. In a place like Liberia, where light and darkness exist side by side, where the darkness is darker than anything I have known and the light is brighter, I hear John announce in his Gospel, "The light shines in the darkness and the darkness cannot overcome it." I want to believe that this is true. That said, my heart wants to know who, why, how. Someone explain to me what these people did and why you don't want to make them pay! Numerous times, when we are alone walking a trail, I press Hosea to help me understand. My questions are dismissed, not with the implication of irrelevance, but with an acknowledgment that everyone needs grace. Perhaps they have stories too dark to tell. Perhaps they have embraced a light too bright for my struggling soul to bear. Hosea's bare feet gently compress the soil on the paths through the forest. My shoes trip on every exposed root.

There is so much more for me to learn. I had always assumed that the rebels must demonstrate how they repented of their senseless cruelty and slaughter. I realized the grace that comes from my heart has a price tag attached to it. My Liberian friends are clear that they have no power over the rebels' hearts, or mine. Today the rebels are mostly disarmed, and the Liberians I know are eager to welcome them back into their communities as a way of insuring a peaceful future. I try to imagine sitting down to a meal with a rebel who has tortured people from my village.

It is too much for my imagination.

Hosea does this after church service every Sunday. Each is clear that grace is a gift that we are not required to earn; it is a gift, not an achievement. These forcefully turning Liberians claim the truth of John's first epistle as their own. "We love because God first loved us…and he has given us this command: Anyone who loves God must also love their brother and sister." They welcome returning rebels as brothers and sisters, not because they are convinced that the rebels' hearts are deeply repentant, but because they have chosen grace so that they might live into a new world. The evidence of this is found in their unrelenting refusal to seek revenge.

When these folks say that the love of our neighbor leads to repentance and repentance leads to grace, they are speaking of a turning that causes them to welcome the rebels who have tortured their families back in the community. In so doing, they do not pretend to understand what lies in the rebels' hearts. Instead they take full responsibility for what lives in their own.

They have taught me these things; reconciliation requires mutuality, but we dare not wait for this mutuality to happen. Forgiveness, offered in the most extreme circumstances, can be one sided. Indeed, there are times when it must be one sided. While their community waits for justice, individuals embrace the grace of forgiveness now. They believe this is required for the reconstruction of their country and their lives.

As I sit on a log with my friend Hosea, we are surrounded by people, yet pay attention only to each other.

His simple question is so hard to answer, "How many pairs of shoes do you own?"

I have no idea. They are on the floor of my closet, in the back of my car, in the garage, under the workbench. I do not know, and even if I did, I could not tell him. He owns nothing except an extra shirt and pair of pants. I lie, and this lie does not require repentance. I tell him that I have two pairs. I cannot say I might have twenty-two pairs.

"How many US dollars do these shoes cost?"

Once again, I lie with a clean conscience and say that they cost ten dollars. The shoes I am giving him today are Columbia low-cut hiking shoes that I bought for this trip. I don't remember how much they cost. Maybe one hundred or one hundred twenty dollars, and I have too many to count. A teacher in John Dean Town makes about ten dollars a week. A fifty-pound bag of rice costs thirty dollars. My material wealth stands in front of my perception of his pure heart, and I feel poverty-stricken. He thanks me, holds them up, wipes them off, and puts them in his bag. Not wanting them to get dirty, he will save them for another day.

I board the flight from Brussels to Newark in my Monrovia street-vendor, blue flip-flops. My feet are cold. I think that I should have kept the pair of socks. Then I repent of my selfishness at such a small, temporary inconvenience. Repentance can be complicated. Do I in any way share responsibility for the nightmare that is Liberia and its war? How about Rwanda, Iraq, wars past, and wars present? What about the children in my neighborhood who are hungry and poorly clothed? What about resentments I have held in my heart: how have they hurt others? I am reminded that while this repentance is important, it is not dependent upon my ability to figure it out and get all things right. What is important is where it leads. Repentance leads to grace and grace leads to generosity.

I am home now, trying to understand the things I experienced. Sliding back from my desk, I reach into a small black, lacquer box and pull out my prayer beads. I rub the opaque, yellow/green bead between my fingers and say, "Repentance leads to grace." This is as far as I can go today. I believe that I know the next step, that grace leads to generosity, and I am committed to going wherever that step takes me.

I hear Hosea ask, "Billy, aren't you a follower of Jesus Christ?" I hear him ask, "How many pairs of shoes do you own?"

Death by Suicide

Sitting in the grass, leaning against the unoccupied bandstand, I looked toward the parking lot and noticed the old, blue, beat-up Ford Fairlane, the car that carried the guys I most admired. When it pulled into a parking place at Riverside Park on Sunday afternoon, they motioned for me to come over. I was a junior in high school, and Riverside Park was the center for local bands and Jackson, Mississippi's fledgling hippy culture. This carload of friends was the epitome of all that Riverside and the folks who hung out there hoped to be. I wanted to be on the inside of their group as much as my questing sixteen-year-old self wanted anything. No matter how hard I tried I had never felt like an insider, here or anywhere else.

The Coolest Guy in the band was in the front passenger's seat, his arm out the window and head cocked as if he were giving directions. It was a joke among our friends that the bass player was the hippest among us, and I suppose he was. When they played, most often in someone's garage, he stood in the back, appearing detached while providing the foundation for the music. The Cool Guy was who I wanted to be, and if I couldn't be him at least I wanted to be in the band. I was a trombone player. Back then, finding a place in a rock and roll band, would have been like wearing a tie to a rock concert. While Chicago, Blood Sweat and Tears, and the horn section with The Silver Bullet Band provided the great exceptions, they were not enough to make a horn-playing band member a heavily recruited musician. Even in the high school marching band, the low brass section was the seat of many an umm pahh pahh, not the seat of coolness. But these guys in the car at the park were tough, independent, bold. Eager to learn, I watched closely and held on tight, wondering if I could ever portray such an image.

On this spring day in the parking lot at Riverside, I was pretty high. Many of us used drugs, but because I wanted so badly to be accepted, I used a greater volume and variety of drugs than most of the other experimenters from my school. Certainly more than these guys. I wasn't sure if they were impressed with my recklessness or not, but I was. I hoped it would prove that I was worthy of their admiration. At the same time, I was anxious more often than not, worried about whether I would fit in or not, worried about getting caught by my parents, though strange as it may seem, I was not thoughtful enough to worry about the police. The anxiety produced in this quest for adventure and my insecure fear of being left out drove me to the cusp of self-destruction.

I had begun to use alcohol in the eighth grade, when some guys in our neighborhood began to sneak bottles from their parents' liquor cabinets. The next summer, another guy just down the street had a cousin come from San Francisco to spend the summer. He had longer hair than we had ever seen on a guy, and he brought albums by bands we had never heard of, as well as a shoebox full of marijuana. We imagined ourselves at Fillmore West as we cranked up the volume on the stereo, listened to the screaming guitars of Santana, Hendrix, and Jimmy Page and learned to smoke weed. While any drug use by a ninth grader is dangerous, mine increased steadily during the next three years. Although my abuse of drugs and alcohol was based on my desire for acceptance, it also seemed purposeful and strangely focused. A natural-born adherent to the idea that something beyond us gave our lives meaning, yet unattached to the faith of my family, I flirted with the idea that drugs provided a path to spiritual insight as well as acceptance by others. My longing to be accepted by The Cool Guy and his friends signaled my belief that they knew something about life that I did not.

Drugs were everywhere, easy to find and not always illegal. I had pulled a muscle in my back while water-skiing earlier in the summer. Our family doctor gave me a prescription for Darvon, and he was willing to keep the prescription filled without asking any probing questions.

"Can you refill my prescription?" I would ask. "Does your back still hurt?"

"Yes, sir, it does." That simple.

In 1969, you could break open the capsule, gently brush away the filler, and find a small, hard ball. The narcotic. I would open a few of these, find the ball in the middle, and take them for a greatly intensified high. No one I knew considered the danger of abusing prescription drugs.

On the day I leaned into the car of The Cool Guy, I had taken three of them and had tossed back at least that many cans of Bud. I put the weight of my body on the car and shoved my head in the front passenger window. The Cool Guy leaned over to make room for me. Jay reached up from the backseat and playfully played a drum riff on my head with his hands. Then The Cool Guy looked at me and said, "Man, you are really messed up." I thought it was a compliment. Then he asked, "Are you taking those pills?" When I said I was, he reached out and took the can of beer from my hand. His long straight hair hung down over his shoulders and hid his face. "Don't be stupid. Mixing that stuff with alcohol will kill you. That's not cool. Pick one or the other." A twinge of gratitude found its way through my foggy brain. Someone was paying enough attention to care what happened to me.

"I'm hip," I said. I had no idea how significant this moment would become.

From that day on, when we were together and I was high, he would ask, "Are you taking pills and drinking?" Regardless of the truth, I always said no and was pleased that he cared enough to ask. Perhaps I, the kid who did not fit in, was just dangerously wild enough that they were actually watching. Maybe I would become one of the people he would call when looking for a friend on a weekend night. How was I to know that his questioning concern would stay with me for the rest of my life? Many decades after I quit using drugs and alcohol, I would still hear the echo of The Cool Guy's voice, concerned about my welfare, a concern that appeared to be deeper than his concern for himself.

One of my primary life tasks would be making peace with that voice.

As I consider what it means to find a way to pray the pathway to peace, I also consider those things that would rob us of peace, the issues that stay with us forever, coloring our view of life itself. Although the intensity of their effect may change over a lifetime, they never go away. Some come with birth, like my particular style of learning and the gifts and challenges it provides. Or the way my damaged heart would take center stage in my adult life. Sometimes the things that would rob us of peace come from outside of ourselves, delivered by the hand of another. The Cool Guy's future, foreseen by none of us, would become one of those things.

Three years after that Sunday afternoon at Riverside Park, I was home from college visiting my parents. A lot can change in three years to a person that young. I had stopped using alcohol or drugs two years since. I had lost touch with most of the guys who seemed important in that previous time. As the young can do, I had reinvented myself. I thought I had left it all behind. Then, unexpectedly, Jay called. My mother spoke out in her always-cheerful voice, "Billy, Jay is on the phone." Jay had been a friend for over a decade, and he was one of the admired cool ones in the car that afternoon at Riverside Park. I picked up the phone in my parents' bedroom. In those days, we thought it was a big deal to have two phones in the house. I would be able to speak to Jay privately on the second phone, from their room in the back of the house.

He offered no preface to the news, but his voice quivered as he said, "The Cool Guy is dead. He took a ton of pills and then drank until he passed out. He choked on his vomit and died in the backseat of his car. Everyone else was high too, so it took them a while to figure it out. They drove to the hospital, but by then it was too late."

The shocking precursor to grief swirled through the room like a tornado. I hung up the phone and began to sob. Pressing a pillow hard against my face, I tried to keep the sounds to myself. I felt ashamed and protective of The Cool Guy. Confused about my shame, I knew that I did not want to discuss this with my parents until I was under control. Immediately, I remembered that afternoon at Riverside Park. I could see The Cool Guy's face as he looked at me and said, "Man, you are really messed up. Are you taking your pills? Don't be stupid. Mixing that stuff with alcohol will kill you. That's not cool."

Who was there to talk straight to him? Not me.

Our friends assumed The Cool Guy's death was suicide. When we got together at a local pizza place, they spoke of how reckless his behavior had become. They told stories of other nights that could have ended just as badly. As they spoke about him, I could imagine his long hair swinging over his face. I could imagine him mixing drugs and alcohol, punching holes in walls during angry outbursts, disappearing for days at a time, driving while stoned out of his mind. Once again, I felt like a foreigner.

Overwhelmed, feeling guilty for being out of touch, I wondered about the night he died: Did he leave home having decided that on this particular night he would die? I have never questioned that thought until I began to write about it. Perhaps it was not that clear. Perhaps he had just quit caring about his life. Did living so recklessly make a night like this inevitable? Had he lost his ability to imagine a hopeful future?

One thing was clear. During the previous three years I had been learning about hope. Between my junior and senior years of high school, I had a dramatic conversion experience. My natural-born believer's heart found a home. On a Wednesday night in July, I sat on the floor of the sanctuary at Alta Woods United Methodist Church with about forty junior high and high school students, pressed into the space between the front row and the altar rail.

The church's youth director, Sam Morris, asked us what we believed would happen if we were to offer our lives, without reserve, to become followers of Jesus Christ. He placed a folding chair in the middle of the group and invited us to sit, one at a time in that chair while the group focused its prayers on us. I remember the warm metal against the back of my legs. He stood behind the chair and reached toward me. I still sense the imprint of his hands on my shoulders as he prayed for me. I have spent the rest of my life trying to find an adequate response to the mystery of that moment. Throughout the night, Randy, Ricky, James, Lynn, Cindy, Susan, my little sister Jennifer all found their way to that chair. It is incredible to note that almost fifty years later the vast majority of these folks remain active followers of their faith.

To speak of religious conversion while avoiding the clichés that have become attached to the faith is extraordinarily difficult.

I could say: It was as if a door opened in the center of my being. That my internal compass swung quickly to true north.

That I experienced a lightness of being, the embrace of a love beyond myself. I could repeat what others have proclaimed:

John Wesley, "My heart was strangely warmed."

Albert Schweitzer, "The real meaning of faith begins at the point at which verbal explanation is inadequate and ceases to be. Yet we know in our inner heart what it is trying to say."

The hymn writer, "My chains fell off, my heart was free, I rose, went forth, and followed…"

It would all be true. These descriptions fit my experience, and I embraced them all as vigorously as I could.

Jesus, who had always seemed appealing, if distant, suddenly felt relationally intimate, alive in the present moment. During the early days of my commitment to Jesus, I spoke primarily of freedom from the burden of myself. I, who had never fit in, felt at home in the universe. While I remained a socially awkward teenager, most at home with my trombone in the low brass section and without the ability to be clearly articulate about this newfound faith, I was free. I experienced an acceptance of myself and others that went along with my perception that I was accepted by God.

This kind of religious experience fit easily into my understanding the world. My family were active members of Alta Woods United Methodist Church, and my parents were insistent that we attend. Our Wesleyan theological tradition relies heavily on the concept of prevenient grace, the idea that God is always prior, active in our lives before we recognize it, preparing us for the future. The tradition of our church was replete with stories of lives offered to God and radically transformed in the aftermath of the moment. On that night, it made sense to me that God had been preparing me for this transformation.

At that time, my life began to shift from being dominated by a struggle to fit in, to embracing a deep desire to express my love of God in service to others. The day after my conversion experience, I cleaned out the drawers in my room and disposed of all my drugs. I waited until my mother left home for work. I didn't want to have to explain the constant flushing of the toilet as I sent various drugs into the sewer system. It occurred to me that it would be a real bummer to get caught with all these drugs on the day I quit using them!

I was not alone. Numerous others who had been present that night told of experiences similar to mine. Together, we quickly moved beyond our parents' insistence that we go to church on Sunday, and we began to meet with others to study the Bible several times a week. We struggled together to understand how to live in a manner consistent with our newfound faith. We searched for ways to be in service to others, feeding the hungry in our community, welcoming the kids in school who were usually left out, and telling stories of transformed lives. We made commitments to each other that satisfied my longing for acceptance and purpose. Naïve but with the heart-felt fervor of true believers, we announced that we would hold each other accountable for our faith. Many of us remain in close contact, struggling with those commitments even now.

That struggle has often been for clarity, a search for how best to keep this commitment of love as it applies to specific circumstances. I have never seriously questioned the validity of the decision I made that night. I have been an ordained United Methodist pastor for over forty years.

I continue to join the members of the congregations I have served in wondering how our relationship with God invites us to come to terms with a crisis like The Cool Guy's death. How do we address powerful life moments over which we have no power except the power of response?

After my conversion experience, the desire for drugs and alcohol vanished. I never used them again. Although I sometimes long for deeper friendships and renewed clarity of my sense of purpose, I have never wanted to see these desires fulfilled in that way. Joining in covenants with others to explore the Jesus way of life by studying scriptures and committing ourselves to following through on our understanding of what it means to be a follower of Jesus: this offered me a sense of where my life was headed.

For a while I kept in touch with some of the old crowd. I had told this story to most of my friends. I told it to The Cool Guy.

One day while we were sitting on the bed in his room, we had turned Zeppelin up loud. He pulled out a joint and lit it. After he took a toke, he reached over to hand it to me.

"No thanks," I said, and I realized I meant it. Cool Guy looked puzzled, "Why not?"

I stuttered and stammered. Yet somehow I managed to tell him that I had become a Christian. I didn't use drugs any longer. He listened politely, even with a mild curiosity, but that was all. After he finished the joint, I did not persist in my explanation of faith. While he continued to express friendly affection for me, he also made it clear that he had no affection for the church and did not care much for Jesus. A significant part of his identity was wrapped up in his rejection of traditional Christian faith. In time, I moved on to another group of friends who shared my newfound commitments.

But in the days following his death, I remembered him, and I tortured myself with questions. Waking up in the middle of a dream, or sitting in the library failing to study, or watching folks walk around on the campus of Millsaps College, I wondered, If I had spoken more clearly, confidently, and consistently about faith with The Cool Guy, would it have mattered? Would he have quit using? Would he have been more careful with his own life? Because I can never know, the question never completely goes away.

The day of his funeral service, I walked into the back of this Southern Baptist church and stood, looking around, not sure where to sit. Finally, I realized I could sit next to Jay on the row reserved for the pallbearers. We would carry The Cool Guy's boxed-up body to its final resting place. Jay's eyes were dilated; he was high. A flash of anger rushed through my veins. Then I stopped; I understood why he would want to dull his senses on this day. For a moment I envied him, and then I began to look around. I saw the pews filled with people who were weeping. The Cool Guy's parents, across the aisle from the pallbearers in pews reserved for family, were devastated at the loss of their son; our friends, scattered throughout the sanctuary, were coming face to face with the consequences of our reckless behavior, each one struggling with their loss or guilt. Each person's grief was unique and devastating, centered on this common loss.

As the pastor began to speak, he told a story of coming to visit The Cool Guy when he was a child, kneeling with him in the living room of their home, and praying as he invited Jesus into his heart. This is the story that triggered both the flow of my own tears and my outrage. How could he say The Cool Guy was a follower of Jesus? Was it because he had knelt with a small child decades before? I gripped the cushion on the pew to resist the urge to stand up and scream! My response sprang from a desire, a longing for truth, not to declare judgment on The Cool Guy, but rather not to have a church leader gloss over the truth. In my presumptuous young mind, everything about this pastor's words lacked integrity. The Cool Guy had respected the way I embraced the Christian faith. He simply didn't buy the story of Jesus, and while he was appreciative of my newfound faith, he assumed it was a passing response to an invisible struggle. His response had been reserved, skeptical, but respectful.

But I did not respect what I considered a lack of integrity on the part of the pastor. My anger toward him came to a rolling boil. It was not until years later that I began to wonder if my judgment of his surety was triggered by the power of my own youthful arrogance. Perhaps I judged the pastor so harshly because he reflected the conceit I embraced. As if I had all the answers. By this point in my life, I knew that I would become a pastor and on that day I vowed that I would not create faith stories to comfort families at funerals. I was certain that no comfort could be found in what I still hold to be this pastor's simplistic, arrogant declaration. It's been over forty years. When will I set him free?

After the funeral, the pallbearers loaded The Cool Guy's casket into the hearse, then Jay's father drove us to the cemetery. We were all young men, but far too distraught to drive ourselves. As we made that awful journey, no one spoke. Finally, Jay's dad offered an assurance that we would be alright. He told us that life was peppered with tragedy and heartbreak as well as goodness. He meant well. It didn't help. His was not the violation of integrity of the pastor, it was simply the clumsiness of a man who had no language for his feelings and certainly no language for ours. I have no further memory of myself or of any of my friends speaking a word all day. Silence wrapped our grief tight in its fist.

As I reflect upon it now, what's finally clear to me is that no person, no words, no expression of empathy could have chipped away at the protective wall erected around my spirit on that day. I possessed a self-righteous anger, born out of a heart longing for a non-existent, merciful world. In retrospect, I am simply grateful that I learned a lesson from the pastor that day. It is a lesson that continues to serve me well even though it was surely not the lesson he intended.

When we arrived at the cemetery, we took seriously our responsibility as pallbearers. We picked up the casket that bore The Cool Guy's defiled body and carried it the short distance between the hearse and the grave. My arms ached as we placed it on the platform above that dark hole where his body would be placed. How could his dead body, abandoned by his spirit, weigh so much? I wanted to speak to his parents, but I did not know them well, and their pain was so visibly intense that I turned away in fear. Perhaps my guilt over our years of reckless behavior made me wonder if they would be too angry to speak to me. Later that night, I wondered who had the courage to offer them kindness. Once, a few years later, while visiting my hometown, I drove past their house. I parked my rental car by the curb and considered knocking on their door. Would they want to be reminded of that dark day? Would they know who I was? Would they want to see me? What would I say?

I turned on the blinker, slipped the car into gear, and drove away. The grief remained evident in my uncertain heart.

As a pastor and during my short tenure as a firefighter, I have encountered many deaths by suicide. Yet there is one more that stays with me, from time to time, keeping me up at night, coupled in some mysterious way to The Cool Guy's death.

A couple of weeks after my fifty-eighth birthday, my sister called. "Billy, Randy shot himself. He is dead."

I could not speak except to stammer, "I'll call you back."

Randy and I had a track of friendship that ran much deeper than my friendship with The Cool Guy. Our parents were close, and he and his brother Ricky were like brothers to me. We grew up in the same church, shared the night of our conversion, and we spent many of our weekends at Lake Cavalier, their family cabin, water skiing, fishing, catching snakes, swimming, and generally acting like Southern boys. All of us were parented freely by each other's parents, Randy's and mine. My sister, the lone girl, and their little brother Scottie, hung onto the edge of every adventure.

As we moved into junior high and high school, Randy and I remained close even as we were evolving different public personas. I wore ratty old t-shirts and ripped jeans. In my memory, he is dressed in pressed Dockers and white polo shirts. Even his jeans had a sharp, clean crease. My mother often admonished me to be more like him. He was the first in everything academic and later received early admission to medical school. He was also the best water-skier in our group. His father spent endless hours driving the ski boat around the lake as we all eagerly waited our turn. In all of this Randy and I never needed to impress each other; our friendship was familial, never evaluated, without struggle, competition, or risk. It simply was.

As we became adults, I sometimes wondered if Randy and his brother Ricky were closer to my parents than I was. This didn't bother me; indeed, it seemed important. My wife and I had moved away from a culture that does not often affirm long moves from home; leaving Mississippi for Alaska and later leaving Alaska for Arizona breaks the proximity rule for our culture. Randy and Ricky had stayed. So it was natural for the relationships to evolve. My parents often acted as wise counselors and comforters to Randy and Ricky. As my parents grew older, Randy and

Ricky, both physicians, took the roles of older sons and helped guide them into life's later stages. Around the time of my father's death, Randy often drove back and forth between Jackson and Oxford, Mississippi. He was relocating his medical practice, and he and his wife, Amy, were building a house in Oxford. It was not unusual for him to call and ask how I was, when I missed my father most, what my fondest memories were. No one else did that. We found comfort in sharing stories of our deceased fathers and the impact they had on our lives.

On the night after he died, Amy called my home in Tucson, Arizona, and asked me to speak at his funeral. I was expecting the call and had already purchased airplane tickets.

These two particular deaths by suicide have become flashpoints in my psyche. Though I live my days in every light I can muster, I sometimes grapple with despair in darkness of the night. Throughout the years, The Cool Guy has come to me in discomforting dreams. On the night of Randy's death, he came with violent beckoning bursts of invitation. And Randy came with him. Come with me. Randy's here. We'll wait for you. It was an invitation I never considered accepting. Still, while I was not afraid that I would join them in death by suicide, I was clearly afraid of the invasion of their despair into the light of my hopeful life. I rose in the bed, swinging my arms and shouting for them to go away. Ann recognized my anguish, as it violated the peace of our night. She had learned to expect these periodic outbursts of undisclosed distress. She reached out to embrace me. "Do you want to talk?"

I apologized for waking her even as I refused her comfort. I did not want to be touched, and I could not think of anything helpful to say to her. When I woke in the morning, I tried to erase these unwelcome visitations from my memory, but they remained, lurking around the edge of the unknown. I continue to struggle between the pull to be embraced by darkness and the desire to flee it too quickly, reaching for the light that cannot be fully embraced as it casts the shadow into the edge of relentless gloom.

When The Cool Guy visits me in this dream state, I am reminded of my funeral practice.

It has been carefully developed over many years of pastoral ministry and maintains the integrity I longed for on the day he was buried; always tell the truth, always end with hope.

Joan Wickersham, in her book, The Suicide Index, speaks of her father's suicide and says, "Suicide is not just a death; it's an accusation. It's a violent public declaration of loneliness. It's a repudiation of connection. It says, 'You weren't enough to keep me here.' It sets up unresolvable dilemmas of culpability and fault: were we to blame for being insufficient, or was he to blame for finding us so? Someone had been weighed and found wanting, but who?"

Wickersham's cry resonates with my spirit as she makes no attempt to clarify the deeper 'why' of suicide, but reaches out to join her lost father in his despair. There are moments, as I wake dreaming in the night, when I hope my dreams will provide a portal from my being 'found wanting' to my ability to accept a full-hearted peace. And just perhaps, by brushing against such despair, I am given a small experience of it. Does it elicit a healing empathy? I'm still learning.

When someone we love dies by suicide, many of us begin with, "It must have been me." At least, that's my first response. It's not reasonable and doesn't stand up to careful examination. When it comes to suicide, nothing does.

I find that I have no answers.

Randy's funeral was held in the sanctuary of First Baptist Church in Jackson, Mississippi, our hometown. Before the service, I stepped into the bathroom. An old friend stood beside me.

"Why did he do it?" he asked.

"I don't know."

"Can he find peace?" he asked. Then he looked at me, as if he expected me to know.

"If grace is true, it's true for all of us," I said.

"Even Randy?"

I responded, "Today, especially Randy."

I stood before the congregation and began with the truth. "I cry. I am not embarrassed by it. You can cry too. My heart is broken. Randy took his life. I do not know why he did it. I do not judge him for it. I do not love him any less. My faith cries out that his life, lived in covenant with God and ended with many broken hearts, has left us with marvelous memories that need not be destroyed by his last horrible hour. I cling to the promise of hope found in Romans: 'Suffering produces endurance, and endurance produces character, and character produces hope, and hope does not disappoint us, because God's love has been poured into our hearts through the Holy Spirit that has been given to us.'"

I told stories of our childhood: his parents and mine at the lake, keeping our mischief barely in check, while we chased ducks across the water and harassed our younger siblings. I looked down at the front row of the church where our mothers sat together, wringing their hands in anguish. The congregation was peppered with friends I had not seen in decades. Calling their names, Bert, Rye, Mike, I spoke of the foolish escapades of our youth. I reminded them of the first night we spent at Lake Cavalier alone. We had felt giddy excitement, as we were trusted with the keys to the house and the keys to the boat without an adult in sight. That night we water-skied by moonlight, ignoring the reprimand we would surely receive if we were caught being so reckless. When a storm blew in, Mr. Russell called for Randy. He didn't want to talk to any of us, only Randy, always the adult. He told Randy to bring the boat out of the water so that it would not be flooded with rain and sink. By the time we got down to the pier, it was the next morning and the towline to the ski boat was pointing straight down, underwater, tied to the sunken symbol of our adolescent disobedience. It took us all day to raise the boat, clean it, and get it on shore.

Sitting in church, looking at each other, our laughter turned to tears. I looked at his son and daughter, just breaking the barrier into adulthood, and remembered that I was their age when we buried The Cool Guy. It would be much harder for them. The sea of faces included Randy's mother, brothers, wife, family, and friends; all of those who counted on him to act responsibly stared back at me. There seemed to be no end to the heartbreak.

"This requires us to take the long view of hope." It always will.

The Cool Guy and Randy still come to me on occasion. Sometimes they come together, sometimes alone. I have asked them not to return. I thrash about in my dream state, throw off the covers, and frighten my gentle wife, Ann. These two very different men abandoned hope for reasons I do not yet and may never, understand. Perhaps none of us can understand such things.

They leave me wondering, *Can others steal my peace? Why do I rehearse their deaths in my imagination as if they were directed toward me? How much do I have to understand before I learn to accept? Can I experience peace and turmoil at the same time?*

I have learned that I can continue to love The Cool Guy and Randy, rubbing shoulders with their despair, while being unable to make peace with the way they died. I can acknowledge that while I still wake in the night thrashing and disturbed by their deaths, I am able to embrace the journey that leads me on the pathway to peace. Both of these inform my life. Neither is easy.

I have come to believe that when Jesus says, "Peace I leave with you. I do not leave it as the world does," he is acknowledging our worldly unease, this human uproar: in the middle of life's most disturbing moments, some moments which may never be complemented by a full explanation or a gentle peace.

Throughout my life as a pastor, I have been intentional in speaking about suicide in church. Each time I do, I am overwhelmed with people who say, "Thank you. I have been haunted by the suicide of my mother, father, child, friend, spouse for decades. No one speaks of it or allows me to." I want to help to remove the taboo from this subject.

The last time I saw Randy's mother, we were in a restaurant with friends. As I helped her to the car, she asked me, "Billy, do you ever think about Randy?"

"Every day," I replied.

She did not smile, but her weary eyes filled with tears as she said, "Thank you," and her eldest son, Ricky, my brother, helped her into the car.

You Are a Miracle

I often begin my day with this simple prayer:

Let me be empty.

Let me be full.

Let me welcome you into my day.

When I offer the words, "Let me welcome you into my day," I am not sure who I want to welcome. It's a prayer, so the answer is God, right? Perhaps, but I never know who I might welcome, who might enter my life hoping for or offering grace.

On what had been an uneventful Monday morning, there was a knock on my office door. I struggle with these unexpected Monday morning knocks. They are not unusual. I have come to know a group of homeless and near-homeless people. And they have come to know how to skip the greeting office. They do not wait to be screened by the administrative staff who work there and shield program staff from unscheduled visitors. Having learned the way in, they slip through the back gate and directly to me. Due to long-standing friendships, they know that they will often come away with more when they skip the office screening and make their case directly to me. They come looking for gasoline coupons, utility and rent assistance, bus passes, school supplies, and food. I know that whatever I do will be genuinely helpful today, but I also realize that many of them will be back tomorrow presenting the same need. The help is immediate and only immediate. For now, this is their life.

That day Erubial came bounding through the door. He possessed possibility these surprise encounters rarely offered. He was an extremely polite, even deferential fellow, so it caught me off guard when he did not wait for an invitation to enter. He rushed through the door, took me in his arms, and announced: "You are a fucking miracle!"

His eyes danced. His voice held no recognizable aggression, only genuine happiness. And of course, his words caught me off guard. No one had ever said that to me before, certainly not in those terms. I am a pastor, and people often apologize to me for their language.

"Oops. Sorry," they will say. "I didn't mean to say that in front of you."

I didn't know how to respond to him. I am generally not offended by the way people speak unless it is hurtful or disrespectful to someone else. So there was nothing offensive in Erubial's words as I replayed them. "You are a fucking miracle!" Not a hint of self-consciousness in his voice. I returned his embrace, thinking, *If there is a miracle in the room, it's not me.* He stepped back, and I invited him to sit down and tell me why, on this particular day, he imagined me to be a miracle.

Erubial and I had first met several months earlier on a Sunday morning. We were at St. Paul's United Methodist Church in Tucson, Arizona, where I was one of the pastors. A member of the church approached me between services and suggested that I speak to a man leaning against the outer wall of a building adjacent to the sanctuary. This was not unusual. I asked people to be on the lookout for first-time visitors, to introduce themselves, and to help me and others on the church staff meet them.

"He's around the corner," my friend said. "You won't miss him." I walked around the corner and yes, our guest was easy to identify, though he may have wished to be less conspicuous. Leaning against the wall, separate from the folks moving on the sidewalk, he was almost hidden from sight. A black hoodie covered his head, and he was smoking a cigarette. Ours is a non-smoking campus, but no one would speak to a visitor about that. We worked hard to create a welcoming environment. As I approached him, I could not see his face and he did not acknowledge me.

"Hello," I said, as I extended my hand. He did not look up or extend his in return. I waited quietly until he spoke, "Is it okay for me to be here?"

"Of course," I said.

"Can I come inside?"

"Yes, the next worship service starts in ten minutes. Come in." I offered my name and extended my hand again. He ignored me and so I walked away. I couldn't help but hope we would find a way to be welcoming to this guest who was as uncomfortable with us as most of our congregation would be with him. A church member who had been watching our exchange told me he would wait for him and help him find a seat. As the service began, he was not in the sanctuary. But after about ten minutes, he walked in and found a seat in the back corner. As we began the last song, he left. He came and went like this for several weeks before we spoke again. In that time I never saw his face and never heard him speak. Occasionally people approached him, but his body language made it clear that he wanted to be left alone.

On a Monday morning I received a call from the outer office. "Billy, there is someone here to see you." Usually, the secretary would send the person down the sidewalk to my office. I could hear the tension in her voice when she said, "I think you will want to come meet him yourself." When asked to come meet someone in the outer office, it often implied that the women working there felt unsafe. I walked down the sidewalk with a quick, anxious gait.

When I walked in, I saw Erubial from behind. I recognized his slight slouch, the black hoodie, his sagging pants, and the underwear sticking out. We often had homeless folks in the office, but it was clear he was not homeless. His clothes were clean, and he had a scent about him that reflected fresh laundry and aftershave. Not many men wear aftershave these days. This man had not been sleeping on the street. As he turned to face me, he pulled his hoodie back. I did not do a very good job of masking my astonishment. Rising from his neck and onto his face were dramatic red and black tattoos. Flames that looked like waves washed around his eyes and onto his forehead. His head was cleanly shaven, revealing dragons whose knife-edged tongues rose from his neck as they licked around his ears and onto his scalp. Drops of blood dripped from the corners of his mouth and eyes.

"It's okay," he said. "The tattoos are supposed to scare you."

"It's working," I said. We both laughed uncomfortably. "Why don't we go to my office where we can talk?"

"Sure," he said. "My name is Erubial."

"Hello, Erubial. My name is Billy."

"I'm not supposed to call you father?" he asked.

"No," I said. "I'm not a priest. Billy is fine."

I pray, sometimes reluctantly, that God will place me in a position to be generous in unexpected ways. Often I believe God does, and I no longer expect it to be on my terms—thus the reluctance. This prayer was being answered the first time Erubial leaned against the wall and waited to see if I would be kind or walk by. Perhaps even then he recognized in both of us the possibility of a miracle.

Let me be empty Let me be full

Let me welcome you into my day.

Erubial and I sat down in my office, and he asked, "Do the things you say in church count for me?" As he said this, he looked at me and said, "I don't know you that well, so I'm not sure."

"I hope they count for everyone," I said.

"That's good, because I can't live like this anymore."

He began to tell me his life story. I noticed that the harsh voice he had used to send me away on the sidewalk that Sunday morning was now soft and kind. It was difficult to reconcile the face of the man sitting before me, and the gentle voice that told his heartbreaking tale.

He told me that he could not remember sleeping more than three hours at a time. "Ever?" I asked.

"Ever," he said. "I sleep with a gun in my hand. I'm a drug dealer. I've always been a drug dealer. I ran away from a foster home when I was nine. I guess no one looked for me. How hard could it be to find a nine-year-old on the streets? A gang took me in and raised me. From the beginning I worked running drugs to earn my keep. They were the only family I had ever known until I met my wife."

Erubial then told me what it had been like for him to meet the woman he married. For the first time, he was treated with kindness and compassion. When they were together, it was not a negotiation. This was different than the code of vengeance that held his gang family together. He discovered that he eagerly embraced his role in protecting her, not wanting to hurt her by the way he lived. She was the only person he knew who he was confident did not want to hurt him or take anything from him.

After their son was born, he would look at him and imagine this little boy sleeping with a gun in his hand. He wanted to know how he could move from the only life he had known to caring for his family.

I had no idea what to say.

He continued to tell me about his life. "I go to work around eleven every night and work until the morning. I'm not lazy. I work hard, and though it may not make sense to you, I am a man of integrity. I am an honest drug dealer. Still, I sleep with a gun in my hand, waiting for some other dealer, some gang banger to break down the door and shoot me. The other night I threw down on my wife. I could have killed her. My kid was standing behind her. I can't do this anymore." Then he wondered what it meant to get a job. *How do I do that? Would you hire me?*

Erubial wanted to explore the possibility of a job beyond dealing drugs and he wanted my help. A paycheck, insurance, and social security seemed an exotic impossibility to him. That made it my job to recognize the possibilities represented by his desire. So while we sat quietly looking at each other, I decided that I must tell him the truth without compromise. He had taken a risk by trusting me. I intended to be worthy of his trust. Where was the possibility in this violent, facially tattooed drug dealer's longing for a new life, and what did justice or grace look like in this case, and did I really believe they would lead to generosity? Will there be justice for him, turned out onto the streets by an uncaring community at such a tender age? Will there be justice for the communities so deeply damaged by him and his gang's violent drug dealing? Beyond all of that, who would consider hiring someone with a face like Erubial's?

As I considered these things, I thought of one of Jesus's lesser-known parables, found in the Gospel of Luke. It is the Friend at Midnight. Suppose an unexpected guest shows up at your home at midnight, but you have no food for that guest. You knock on your neighbor's door, asking for bread and cheese. Your neighbor, angry that you've woken the children, sends you away. You refuse to leave, continuing to knock, until finally, not out of love but desperation, the neighbor gives you what you ask so you will go away.

It occurred to me that if Erubial were to get a job, it would require this kind of persistence.

Let me be empty; let me be full.

I was feeling empty of ideas at that particular moment.

"How do I get a job?" he asked again. "Look at my face. Would you hire me?"

"No, I wouldn't hire you." The moment's honesty was leading me to feel even emptier. "So what do I do?"

I thought, *Lord, let me be full.*

"You get a job. Any job. You do that job so well that someone begins to trust you. Then you get a better job."

"Do you really believe that?" he asked.

"I don't think you have any other choice."

Over time we developed a job-finding strategy. It was clear that he used his voice, language, and tone, to control the atmosphere around him. Like removing his hoodie to reveal his facial tattoos, he could turn his harsh voice on and any reasonable person would back down. At the same time, responding to cues I didn't recognize, his voice could become gentle and calm, and the feeling in the room would change. He had this power, was quite aware of its impact, and considered it a necessary job skill for a successful drug dealer. Intimidate people so they will back down, or bring calm to a situation so the violence will not escalate.

So we talked about the tone required to lessen intimidation and how to speak to a potential employer about a job. His language was peppered with curse words. He underestimated their effect and the impact they had on others. They would not be helpful in a job interview, so we made a list of words he could not use. You can make that list in your imagination now. We came up with a list of nine and began to use substitute words that were intended to create a gentler presentation. For many words there was no effective substitute, so I simply said, "Just don't say that anymore."

He understood this immediately. "I'm scary looking, and I talk this way to become even more intimidating. To get a job I must become less frightening. I'm a good drug dealer, so nobody is going to—" he stopped and searched his imagination for a replacement for one of the newly forbidden words. He looked at me and substituted, "—bother me. No one is going to bother me. I can only get a job if somebody is no longer afraid." His unusual intelligence became clear as he successfully practiced finding synonyms in his second language.

We talked about how he would dress and what time of day would be best for making applications. He began to get up every morning believing that it was his job to find a job. He went from place to place, up and down the main thoroughfare in our part of the city. Mostly fast-food places. Almost everyone said that they had no openings, yet he politely insisted that they give him an application. He would fill it out and turn it in. No one called.

Let me welcome you into my day.

The next week he followed up by going to each one of them again. Like the friend at midnight, he did this day after day, week after week. He quit working the streets at night, telling his gang he would no longer sell drugs. While they didn't do anything to help him, they didn't try to stop him either. It felt like they were as on his side as they could be, unspoken allies watching their compatriot make the break.

He came to see me weekly. Every Monday in the early afternoon. "Do you really believe this is going to work?" he would ask each time.

"Yes, I do."

Then he would ask, "Will you pray with me?"

"Yes, we can pray together."

I wanted to believe that he could create a new life for himself and his family. If I didn't believe it, then what was I doing with my life? Surely, I didn't stand up each Sunday and announce a hope I didn't believe existed. Could it be that the strength of my faith hinged on a lifetime drug dealer who was hoping to turn into a respectable fast-food worker? But if the promise of new life didn't have meaning for Erubial, then it had no meaning for me. As he was leaving my office one day, he reached in his pocket and pulled out a wad of bills. "I want to buy a Bible," he said.

"I have plenty of Bibles. Is it okay if I give you one?"

"Will you write in it?" I didn't understand what he wanted, so I said that he would have to tell me what he wanted me to write. "Please write, Erubial was given this Bible by Billy, the pastor of the church. That way no one will think that I stole it."

Let me be full.

I wrote the message just as he asked, yet I was sad that he had been treated so poorly that this was required. Erubial had a practical view of the world that was impressive and totally absent of self-pity. He understood that all of us took one look at him and assumed the worst. I also understood this was a complex transition for him. While he was considered a leader in his gang-dominated drug culture, he was also a naive immigrant struggling to find a place in this new culture of jobs and nonviolent families. He was even learning a new kind of English as his third language.

After a while, Erubial quit coming to church on Sunday, but he kept coming to see me every Monday. When I asked him about it, he told me he had begun to worship in a Pentecostal Church where the worship was in Spanish and things were livelier. He wondered if I would be angry. I was not.

"Can I still come see you on Mondays?" he asked.

"Of course."

"Do you still believe I can find a job?"

I took a deep breath and looked inside my heart. Thinking of the widow crying for justice to the callused judge, I had to tell the truth. "I do. It's going to be hard. But don't quit. You will find a job and then you will find a better job."

"Do you still believe that I can leave my world and come to another one?" I didn't flinch this time. "Yes, I do."

Jesus's parable of persistence ends with the question: How much more do I have to ask? If the neighbor and judge will help you, just to get you to go away, how much more will God, who loves you, act on your behalf? "Ask and you will receive. Seek and you will find. Knock and the door will be open." Sometimes, it takes a while.

This is the place we are invited to work tirelessly to reimagine the church as well as civil institutions and to hold them accountable for their responses to the most vulnerable in our society. We are also called to a fearless moral inventory of our own lives. Although we may work tirelessly to affect the larger institutions of power, I know Erubial cannot wait. He is crying out for someone to care now.

Let me welcome you into my day

It is easy to confuse the macro and micro answers to these deepest human needs. Going door-to-door looking for a minimum wage job is not the answer to high unemployment or the scourge of drugs among the poor. This simplistic response will not be the answer for all the Erubials in the world. Gangs that terrorize neighborhoods are not going to clear the streets and begin looking for jobs at Taco Bell. Systematic change is required to create communities where children cannot walk away from foster care only to find that they are quickly forgotten. Persistently beating on the doors of the powerful while demanding justice will not solve the problem of poor education, health care, and the isolating loneliness that causes us to move through life in a state of desperation.

However, when you look across your office at one person named Erubial, who says, "I can't live like this anymore," you cannot ask him to wait. You must reach deep into the heart of faith and say, 'Yes, you can create a new life. Yes, I believe in you. Yes, there is a place for you in the heart of God. And yes, if you keep knocking on my door, I will answer it.' On that day the answer is to say, "Erubial, believe in yourself. Hit the streets and get a job."

I say all of this, repeating it in my sacred imagination. I believe that it speaks to the depth of human possibility. At the same time, I do understand that it simply might not work. Why would anyone choose to place Erubial behind the counter in their restaurant? How long will he persist in knocking on doors that remain closed to him? How many hungry nights must pass before he, overwhelmed with discouragement, picks up his gun and heads back into the streets? Will a brave, faithful, compassionate business owner look up and open the door for this man before it is too late?

Mother Teresa often said, "The work we do is no more than a drop in the ocean, but without it the ocean would be one drop less." Me and Erubial, a drop in the ocean. As he leaves my office, I reach into the small decorative box on my desk that houses my prayer beads. I pick them up and roll them between my fingers, praying as I move gently from one to the other.

Prayer begins with silence

Silence leads to the love of God

The love of God leads to the love of neighbor

The love of neighbor leads to repentance

Repentance leads to grace

Grace leads to generosity

Generosity leads to peace

Erubial continued to come and see me from time to time. On the day he burst into the room and without hesitation grabbed me and declared me to be a miracle, he had come to say this at last, "I got a job. I make burritos. I have to work in the back. They won't let me work up front. I might scare off the customers, you know."

"Yes," I said as we both laughed. "I do know."

After that, I did not see him again for several months. Then one day he knocked on my office door. As he entered, I noticed that when we greeted each other, he held himself differently. He no longer slouched, his hoodie did not cover his head, his pants were pulled too high for his underwear to show, and he had a big smile on his face as he announced again, "You are a miracle!"

"It seems to me that you are the miracle."

He laughed. "My boss at the burrito place buys old houses and flips them. I have been working with him on my days off. It seems I'm good with tools, and I like using them."

"He has begun to trust you," I said tentatively, hoping I was right.

"At the burrito place, I always come to work early and stay late. When he asks me to do something, I do it right away. I never complain, and I do it right. He trusts me, and so I am going to run one of his remodeling crews. As part of my pay, my family gets to live in a house he owns. No more burritos and hiding in the back."

I said, "So why am I a miracle?"

"It took a miracle for you to believe in me. It took a miracle for me to believe in you!" he paused, assessing the words, "I guess we are a miracle."

"I guess so. Thank you, my friend."

Erubial may not have known it, but he saw the miracles of possibility in his life. He saw them in me, in himself, in his wife and children, in the freedom to sleep without a gun in his hand, in a job making burritos, and in the possibility of a better job and a new life. He invited me to see them, too.

Like the friend at midnight, Erubial demanded justice for himself so that he could be generous with others. His heart instinctively embraced the possibility of grace that leads to a new life. His friendship helped me to once again see clearly the possibilities of grace alive in the lives of surprising people. While insisting on developing a continuing relationship with me, Erubial created the opportunity to clarify and reaffirm my most important beliefs. He was an answer to my often-prayed prayer.

The gift of his presence in my life invited me to remember that the grace we receive, beautiful as it is, must lead us somewhere. If it is to live, it must lead us to lives of generosity.

Jesus ends the parable of the persistent friend at midnight by saying, "Ask, and it will be given you; search, and you will find; knock, and the door will be opened for you."

I ended my time with Erubial when he walked out of my office door with hope. Were we miracles to each other? We were two people who recognized that the unearned gift of grace leads us to lives of generosity. That is a miracle. Where would it lead us now?

Let me be empty. Let me be full.

Let me welcome you into my day.

There Is No Place I Would Rather Be

On those rare occasions when I think I am going to die I find myself looking across the bow of a kayak or canoe, or I'm at the end of a rope on a backcountry ski slope, or I'm probing for crevasses, or digging a snow pit in a blizzard. And in the midst of fear and anxiety, I find my view of impending doom is obscured by my friend Will. Whether on Mount Logan, in Liberia, or kayaking blindly into towering ocean waves, there he is, blocking my view, impatient, ready to move, and seemingly oblivious to the danger ahead. His eagerness for adventure, even peril, and his competence in the backcountry make me keen to join him time and time again—even when I wonder if this moment may be our last!

Before I signed up to race Dyea to Dawson, I knew he would be there, blocking my view.

I was sitting on the front steps of my house, scanning the Anchorage Daily News when I found this small notice buried in the metro section.

Dyea to Dawson. In celebration of the one hundredth anniversary of the Klondike Gold Rush fifty teams will re-enact the race to the Klondike. These fifty teams of two must be residents of either Alaska or the Yukon Territory. Each participant will be required to carry a minimum of fifty pounds of prescribed Gold Rush gear as they race over the Chilkoot Pass into Canada, canoe the headwater lakes of the Yukon River and the Yukon itself to Whitehorse and then on to Dawson City. Only those who are highly skilled in wilderness travel and survival need apply. The dangers will be great and the suffering immense. Participants will have a maximum of fourteen days to complete this wilderness journey of approximately 700 miles. Entry fee is $600. Yo Ho the Yukon!

I didn't bother to call Will; he was traveling in Germany. I also knew he would say yes. In those pre-internet days, I called for a copy of the application. It arrived in the mail a few days later. I filled it out for both of us, wrote our check, signed our names, and registered that day. When Will returned, he came by the house. I told him about the race and that he owed me $300 for his part of the entrance fee. Ann rolled her eyes and chuckled as she offered a resigned sigh.

"I've always wanted to do that trip but never had the time," Will said. "This way, it won't take so long; we'll just go!" And then he uttered those poorly considered words that spell disaster for many an adventurer who has already make up their mind to just go, "How hard could it be?"

"Don't you want to know when it is?" I asked.

"It must be in the summer sometime. Does it matter?" I laughed and said, "I'll call you with the dates."

It was 1996. I was in my early forties and Will was ten years older. Long ago we had settled on lives punctuated by big adventure.

For this particular adventure, Ann, chief negotiator for tempering our recklessness, sat on the sidelines and shook her head in wonder. I should say something about Ann. Over time, she has made her peace with these exploits, as she finds herself caught somewhere between enthusiasm and terror. Our trip to Mount Logan and the brief tension it created had long passed. We had made our peace with my desire to go to wild places and her anxiety about life's more basic concerns. By this point, Ann and I had come to a place of acceptance, understanding that we do not ask each other permission. We consult as to time, schedules, and money. Both of us take the opportunity to express our interests and concerns, and then we affirm each other's decisions. We have become generous with one another, offering our blessing to the other one's longing. It is rare for one of us to object to the other one's strong desire. Still, she cannot help but question how much my friends and I really know about what we are doing, while simultaneously acknowledging that we are highly skilled, as well as much happier, more creative, and easier to get along with when adventure is on the horizon. Pushing myself to the limits of skill, strength, knowledge, and ability makes me a much more interesting and amicable companion. Through the eyes of adventure, my world is expanded, boundaries pushed back and obstacles removed. Being outdoors and challenged opens the eyes of my heart, and I become God-alive, vigorous, and full of hope and possibility. Without it, my life becomes dull, colorless, and flat. Knowing this causes Ann to practice extreme generosity in these matters. This generosity rises out of the movement of grace that thrusts us forward, free of competition and curious about the future. It is a generosity that leads us to a mutual peace.

As I have examined my life of adventure, friendship, and those odd encounters that shape me, I have also explored what it looks like to pray in this particular pattern—one that leads me to peace. I have spent very little time talking about meditation or various prayer practices. In Paul's first letter to the Church in Thessalonica, he instructs the people to: "Be cheerful no matter what; pray all the time; thank God no matter what happens…"

The only way I know to do this is to allow the movement of my body to be a prayer. Prayer for me is an expression of the active life. I am better able to be generous with myself and others if I focus on the movement of the moment. This is a generosity that leads me to peace.

This dynamic, that grace leads to generosity, and generosity to peace, is a vivid reminder that the spiritual life is not stagnant or stale. When in motion, it is vital and alive. This comes to life for me most vigorously when I am out-of-doors, my body in motion. Here the tension in generosity is expressed, as I am compelled to release that to which I hold most tightly, control. When moving in the wilderness I am required to give up my resistance, enter into the flow of the physical landscape, and if I have companions, surrender any sense of competition so that we might become partners in exploration. Examining peace while traveling with a companion, especially one like Will, over glaciated mountain passes and headed down the mighty Yukon, I have learned this peace is not gentle, quiet, or without threat. It is a peace that is embraced in a storm and is not denied its power by the uncertain tumult that surrounds us. These storms are defined by wind, rain, the onset of disease, and the presence of those who love us well, those who do not, and those who don't care.

While Will and I did not know how to say these things to each other, decades of mutual adventure-seeking caused me to believe that they were understood. We were restless; it was time to feed our hunger once again. We were going to the Klondike, and while unsure of what we would find, we were confident beyond reason that adventure and its dangerous peace were waiting on the horizon and we would find it.

We had no hope of winning: we simply wanted to finish within the required fourteen-day limit. After all, even though we sought adventure, we were not competitive racers. The $5,000 in gold coins that awaited the first team to finish would not fund our trip. Then the inevitable happened. We began to read articles about others who had entered the race. Olympians, well-known mountain guides, and some of Alaska and Canada's most renowned adventurers. While we had no illusions of winning, we didn't want to be last, either. We renegotiated our thinking, this time with a twelve-day trip in mind. Only when we arrived in Skagway, Alaska, for the pre-event meetings, did we begin to wonder if we were in over our heads.

Standing around talking on the streets of Skagway, I overheard a conversation that clarified for me who our competitors were and what we had gotten into.

"How many miles did you race in your canoe last year?" one guy asked another.

"It's been a hard year. We haven't had much time to get away. Maybe 1500 miles?"

They turned to me. "How about you?"

"Oh," I stammered. "We haven't raced any, but I have been in a canoe, maybe 500 miles."

I clarified, ahem, "Lifetime."

They gave me an incredulous glare. "You and your teammate did these 500 miles together, I suppose?" one asked.

I gulped and told the truth, "My partner and I have never been in a canoe together. Mostly we kayak."

The group laughed and one guy said, "This may be a tough place to learn. If you finish, you will know a lot more than you do today. If you don't, we will come to your memorial and say that you were foolish, yet brave."

I looked through the crowd and captured a glimpse of Will's childlike, eager, sheepish grin. He and I wandered around, looking at the canoes being loaded on the train that would take them around the mountain to the shore of Lake Bennett where we would pick them up. A long climb over the glaciated Chilkoot Pass would remind us of the deep suffering endured by the original Klondike Goldrushers. After that, our canoes would be waiting for us. We felt uneasy as we read the words printed on their sides.

Sponsored by REI
Sponsored by the National Geographic Society
Sponsored by the Canadian Broadcasting
Corporation
Sponsored by the Australian Geographic Society
Sponsored by Old Town Canoes

And more.

A cameraman from the Canadian Broadcasting Company approached us. He told us that he was making a documentary of the race and asked if he could interview us.

"Who is your sponsor?" he asked.

Will and I looked at each other, and then Will responded, "Our wives. They pay for us to leave home a couple of weeks a year."

"No, really," he said.

"No, really. We have no sponsor. We are just happy to be here."

We returned to our room and spent the rest of the day throwing away excess gear, getting our packs down to the absolute minimum required weight of 50 pounds, and revising, again, our race schedule. Now we reduced the time we were allowing ourselves to ten days. Ten days is a long time to suffer, if you are a couple of urban Alaskans with graduate degrees and office jobs. Although we spent a lot of time in the outdoors, we hardly compared with the professionals who would be traveling beside us. We were eager, excited, still unafraid, and utterly willing to ignore many truths about what lay ahead.

Early the next morning we stood in the starting corral waiting for our chance to begin. The trail was too narrow for a mass start so, in an order determined by lottery, they called each team's name and then competitors took off at two-minute intervals, headed up the trail that would lead over the Chilkoot Pass to a checkpoint thirty-five miles away and staffed by Canadian Mounties in their Dudley Do-Right finest. I looked to my right and noticed that I was standing beside Vern Tejos, the only person to solo Denali and Mount Logan in the winter and survive. Few people alive have endured the level of suffering he did on those climbs. I cannot imagine anyone else whose skill level in the outdoors approaches his. He appeared to be happy, jovial, and eager to go, confident that he and his partner would go home weighed down with $5,000 in gold coins. If I had known then that they would barely break into the top ten, finishing ninth, I might have packed up and called it a day. I naively believed that with people like Tejos toeing the starting line, the rest of the crowd was racing for second. Perhaps I was not the only one underestimating the difficulty of this event.

The first day was easier than I anticipated. Will and I charged up the mountain for a mandatory camp out. Glaciers glittered on the horizon and mud sucked at our feet. We would restart the next morning after coffee and oatmeal, not knowing how rare a simple, cooked meal would soon become. Until we arrived at the very end, about 650 miles distant, this was the only day of the race with a finish line.

On the second day, we left the starting line, one team at a time, in the order of the previous day's finish. For the first time, it was obvious who was leading the race. We found ourselves somewhere in the middle of the pack, which was quite encouraging for us. At the pass that marked the US/Canadian Border, the Mounties took the same role they took in the original gold rush. They checked each person's equipment to be sure we had the required gear. During the original gold rush, they wanted to be sure you had enough gear to survive for a year, if you lived that long.

Many didn't.

The jury was still out on us.

Included in the gear each racer was required to carry was five pounds of beans. A bit of levity took the day when one team said to the Mounties, "They didn't say what kind of beans. They just said five pounds of beans." They had each packed five pounds of jellybeans. We laughed and passed them around as each of us took a handful. Their packs were now five pounds lighter, and we were all smiling.

Then it began to rain. And to freeze. The freezing rain fell in thick, heavy sheets that drove us to relentless forward motion because we became, in short order, too cold to stop.

Charging down the muddy, mountainous, single-track trail, we arrived at the abandoned train station on the shores of Lake Bennett. It was a disturbing scene. Sleep deprivation, nutritional depletion, and pouring rain were already taking their toll. People were lying around, shivering in their sleeping bags. After a quick meal, I decided to take a nap. Just as I dozed off, my bag began to slide across the floor. I jumped up in anger to find Will tugging on the end, trying to shake me out.

"Get up! Get up now! There are only four canoes left by the lake. If we don't hurry, we are going to be last."

We were only a day and a half into the race. It was far too early for a slow team like ours to concede last place. I got up, stuffed my gear in my pack, and headed out to the canoes. Will pointed anxiously to our canoe and he was correct. It was in a row of four. However, behind it was another row of ten and behind that another row. Blinded by eager anxiety, he could not see anyone's boat but ours.

"Well," he said. "We are already up. We might as well go."

We struck out into the darkest part of the Yukon night and began crossing a series of about 150 miles of connected lakes. It felt like paddling across the ocean. Icy cold waves washed over the bow of our boat. It was a sensation that would never become comfortable but would become familiar. Although we had not spent much time in a canoe, we had spent many days in a kayak. We knew the basic principles of paddling through big waves. Keep your boat at a forty-five-degree angle. Do not point it directly into the wave or it will knock you back and perhaps over. Do not let your boat become parallel to the wave or it will roll over, for sure. By this point we were a couple of miles from shore, the water was brutally cold, the waves were up. Our primary goal: do not flip the canoe. Not only would that signal the end of the race, it could very well be the end of us. People die on trips like this.

While blocking the view in front, Will did manage to turn around, offer a big goofy grin, and shout, "What a great day!"

We had reviewed the maps and had seen a confusing configuration of glaciers, mountains, wind, and water called Windy Arm and Sucker's Cove. Windy Arm was the place where two inlets of water flowed out of tidal glaciers and formed a V pattern which merged into the larger lake. Sucker's Cove was the cove at the point of this V shaped configuration. High winds roaring off glaciers came into the arm, each generating large waves. When the waves met in the middle they created haystacks of water, some up to six feet high. By then it was past midnight, and though we were tired, depleted, and cold, we assumed this would be our condition for many days to come. We had made friends with a team from Juneau, Dirk Miller, and Derek Peterson. Dirk and Derek followed us part of the way across the Arm and then, wary of the growing haystacks, the cold and the dark, turned back and waited for daylight. Riddled with doubt, Will and I were not confident enough to believe we could safely turn our boat around so we pushed forward, deciding to head into Sucker's Cove so we would be closer to shore. That way, if our boat should flip, we would probably make it to shore before hypothermia set in and we drowned.

That was our well-considered theory.

It was not well considered enough. While our friends were far behind, waiting for the wind to die down, Will and I found that we could not paddle out of Sucker's Cove. The raging waves crashing on the shore were too strong. Eventually we gave up, pulled our boat on shore, and portaged for several exhausting miles around the cove. Later, when we told this story to some Mounties, they broke out laughing and said, "They call it Sucker's Cove for a reason, eh?"

This would not be the last time the wind, rain, currents, and the illusion of safety would draw us into a place where our escape was not assured. After crossing Lake Bennett, we still had Tagish and Marsh Lakes to cross before we reached the Yukon River. These lakes offered a combined distance of about seventy-five miles. Open water crossings that long, in a canoe, were physically and emotionally devastating. They were also frightening at times, and yes, one can get lost on a lake. More than one team found themselves fooled by a cove that seemed to offer safety but also added ten or twenty miles to their trip. The level of sleep-deprived discouragement that came from an additional seven to ten hours added to the crossing of each lake breaks the will, crushes one's spirit, and freezes the mind. Will and I avoided these detours, not due to skill but sheer persistence. We simply struck out across the middle and refused to surrender to the likes of Sucker's Cove again.

The end of Marsh Lake is the beginning of the Yukon River. In our imaginations, it had a distinct beginning with a smooth but rapid current that would sweep us into Whitehorse, Canada, and a required twelve-hour layover. Another surprise. The transition from the lake to the river was indistinct, current free, miles wide, flat, discouraging, and slow. With no visible current moving the surface of the water, we sat, paddles across our laps, unmoving and unmotivated, discouraged and tired. We recognized that it did seem, at least for the moment, safe. We pulled over to a sand bar, cranked up our stove, and ate. And ate and ate. Old stale bagels smeared with peanut butter and chunks of cheese. Anything that promised to come to life in boiling water. Oatmeal, dried fruit, macaroni and cheese, hot chocolate, instant coffee. No thought was given to what pairs well. We were on a quest for calories and volume.

Soon our friends Derek and Dirk joined us for this 'gourmet' meal. When packing, they had decided that the best way to get the most calories, the lightest weight, and the easiest preparation was freeze-dried mashed potatoes. They were proud of their creative bagging effort, a different type of spice added to each bag. Like us, they were not thinking of a race; they were thinking of a trip. But so far, we were traveling an average of twenty-one hours a day. That meant most meals were consumed on the water, grabbing handfuls of food as we paddled. I will never lose the image of Dirk and Derek, floating across a lake or down the Yukon River, shaking ziplock bags of freeze-dried potatoes into their mouths. They each had a consistent rim of white powder encircling their stubble of beards.

We left our potato-mouthed pals and plowed through the first miles of the Yukon River as it led us to Whitehorse, a required twelve-hour layover and preparation for the crossing of Lake Laberge. One would think that the required layover in Whitehorse would be a respite of uninterrupted sleep. One would be wrong. Our bodies twitched with nervous energy. Our minds raced ahead, wondering what we would find as we crossed Lake Laberge. Sleep was intermittent and devoid of peace.

Later, Dirk and Derek arrived at the campground and noisily woke us up. We all headed into Whitehorse, where we ate breakfast, and our friends ate potatoes that were fried and not crushed into powder in a Baggie. This also became a place to receive valuable information about Lake Laberge, which loomed in our imagination like the terror it would become. At fifty kilometers in length and over five kilometers wide, it was a return to big open water, carrying with it the likelihood of strong winds, rain, and cold angry waves. Or it could be no more than a long, gentle slog. There was no way to know, and we were too tired to think carefully about any of this.

But our waiter was eager to offer advice. "The winds often cease at midnight. When you get back into the river, below the lake, stay away from the shore. It's easy to get lost."

I thought, *How do you get lost on a river? Just float downstream. Right?*

I might be considered a slow learner.

When we arrived at the entrance to Lake Laberge, the wind howled and the rain poured down. A large group of racers huddled around a roaring campfire. No one was willing to take a canoe into this maelstrom. Certainly not Will or me. We laughed and took turns trying to remember Robert Service's poem, *The Cremation of Sam Magee*. This was as far as our collective memory would go,

There are strange things done in the midnight sun

By the men who moil for gold;

The Arctic trails have their secret tales

221

That would make your blood run cold;

The Northern Lights have seen queer sights,

But the queerest they ever did see

Was that night on the marge of Lake Laberge

When I cremated Sam McGee.

It happened in an instant; the wind and the rain stopped. I looked at my watch. Midnight. Just as our Whitehorse friend had told us. Before anyone could comment on the change in the weather, Will and I climbed in our boat and hit the lake. Derek and Dirk were close behind and would soon catch up.

If you have spent much time in a boat, you will recognize the joy that comes when the water is glassy smooth and the wind is in your favor. This was that moment. We could hear our canoe slicing through the thirty-seven-degree, Lake Laberge water. Perhaps for the first time, we felt confident and strong. We fearlessly struck out through the middle, the most direct route. Assuming we did not stop and that the weather remained this calm, we'd share an uneventful eight to ten hours across the lake. No stopping. We could do this.

I cannot help but reflect on the old adage, "To assume is to make an ass out of you and me." We put our confidently assuming heads down and paddled. No thought to the future, only the moment—and for the moment, the moment was good.

We used, as a marker, a large outcropping of rock in the distance. I do not know how far away it was. I only know that finally, to avoid discouragement, I had to look in another direction. After paddling for hours, it never appeared any closer. This was a cruel optical illusion, and yet, unreasonably, our confidence continued to rise. Now Dirk and Derek were beside us in the water. We were moving in tandem, as fast as we had at any point of the race. With a gentle wind at our back, urging us forward, hope dominated our imaginations. We allowed ourselves to be lulled into this lazy thinking: we would cruise easily and swiftly for the rest of the race. We embraced a dangerous peace.

One minute the lake gentled our canoe over a smooth surface. We thought ourselves highly skilled canoeists moving at a rapid pace. Then, Lake Laberge revealed her cruel intention. Without warning, the wind shifted. A wave of icy, chilled water washed over the bow of our canoe and all forward progress stopped. The sky turned an ominous gray and clouds swirled in undistinguishable patterns. Waves rose higher, roaring in our direction. Every fifth or sixth one rose above the bow of our canoe and dumped its cold icy deposit in our laps. Hoping to see relief on another horizon, I turned around to examine what the lake looked like behind us and my view was obscured by my companion, Will: a familiar moment, one where I wondered if we had the skill or the luck to get out of it. My mind was moving rapidly toward a blank slate, eager to just do my job. Will was smiling. The moon peaked out of the clouds over his shoulder.

If you choose to do battle with the storm, you will lose. You must come to understand its movements, as you seek an alliance with the earth itself. So I paddled a prayer. Keep the boat pointed at a forty-five-degree angle into the waves, paddle with a deep, consistent motion, feel your shoulders burning, and try not to imagine that you must keep this up for hours, many hours. Perhaps the intensity of focus caused me to receive Derek's voice with a disconcerting frustration.

"Do you know where I wish I was right now?"

My interior monologue screamed, No and I don't care. Shut up and paddle!

Derek did not wait for a response. He rarely does. "All I want is to be right here, right now, in this boat, beside you guys, in this storm, beside that rock outcropping, making very little progress. This is perfect."

I wish I had said that. I wish I had thought that. I wish I had believed that. At that instant, filled with dangerous possibility, this phrase attached itself to my longing for peace in a manner that can only be found through generous surrender to the moment. This awareness invited me to plough through the wet, gray, bitterly cold moment and a thousand after that, and a thousand other challenging moments since then. So I paddled and I cried out then and now, "All I want is to be right here, right now."

So I no longer resist. I cannot defeat a mountain, or a river, a lake, or a storm. The best I can do is surrender to the flow of the moment, as I trust the world that surrounds me. During moments like this one, when Lake Laberge unleashes her unrelenting fury, I want to become part of the fury, unafraid, racing ahead and willing to accept the consequences. I am not afraid, I just don't want it to end. I find it life giving to act as if this moment is the best moment of my life. Who knows? It might be. This dangerous peace settles my soul.

The second required layover in the race called for an eight-hour rest at Fort Selkirk, a small village on the banks of the Yukon after you exit Lake Laberge. Even in our severely compromised state, Dirk, a schoolteacher, freelance writer, and AP reporter, managed to hang on to his sense of humor. While in Fort Selkirk he posted this story. It ran in newspapers all across the United States and Canada.

The Juneau team of Derek Peterson and Dirk Miller looked everywhere to find an advantage. After watching a particularly turbulent section of Taglish Lake just outside of Carcross Yukon Territory turn placid in front of a canoe paddled by Billy Still and Will Miles of Anchorage, the local pair decided to follow.

On a break a short time later, Peterson and Miller discovered what they believed to be the Anchorage team's secret—divine intervention. Turns out Still is a United Methodist minister, and for the remaining 500 miles to the finish line, the Juneauites never traveled too far from Still and Miles.

Reports of them walking across Lake Laberge are still unconfirmed.

Will and I finished the race in 8:14:39:26, far ahead of any pre-race predictions. There were fifty starting teams and thirty-eight finishers. We finished number thirty-four. Dirk and Derek, who were to become lifetime friends, finished thirty-three, in 8:14:38:50. They said they dug deep and swept past us in the end. We said we lifted our paddles out of the water and let them glide in ahead of us. In reality, none of us were thinking clearly enough to care. In the spirit of the Gold Rush, we were required to drive a post in the ground to stake our claim. We stumbled up the rocky slope and found that with our paddle-weary arms, a stake and a sledgehammer, we could barely break ground.

The next morning I woke up alone. I was wrapped in a sleeping bag in the back of a windowless van, on the side of the road, in Dawson City. It was not my van and not my sleeping bag. Exhaustion had so thoroughly taken over that I had no memory of how I got there. I could not find any of my gear, not even our boat. By some act of luck, grace, or intention, my billfold was lying on the van floor beside me. I walked into Dawson City alone, stopping to call Ann and let her know that the journey was over; we made it safely and would be home in a few days.

"Billy, I love you and I'm glad you finished. Are you alone?"

"Yes, why do you ask?"

"Because you called me and told me all of this last night. Don't you remember?"

"Yes, of course," I lied.

"Maybe you could find some of your friends and hang out with them." Is she making fun of me? Is she worried about me? I have no idea where my friends are.

After I hung up I headed down the boardwalk and into Klondike Kate's, where I ordered The Miner's breakfast. When I finished, I stepped out onto the sidewalk and saw Will, Dirk, Derek, and another guy coming in. I joined them, and to the waitresses' delight, I ordered The Miner's breakfast again. It did not seem possible that my depleted body would ever store enough food to bring me back to life.

Journeys like this require a sense of generosity that dominates each decision. I can't travel in the wilderness for eight and a half days, moving an average of twenty-one hours a day, preparing food for an hour, and sleeping two hours, without experiencing the need to offer and receive grace. Peace cannot be contingent on the quality of performance. While in stressful and even life-threatening situations, I allow myself to be embraced by a generosity born of grace that leads to the peace that "the world cannot give and the world cannot take away". I lose touch with this peace during times of lethargy, not times of crisis. Yes, I am learning to pray without ceasing in the still and quiet. And also in movement. For me, it is simply more natural to pray without ceasing when I move. Adventure, new people, new places, danger, intense physicality, all heighten my senses and sharpen the edges of my spirit. These experiences invite me to quiet the turmoil that rages inside me and to become aware that prayer begins with silence, and enhances and inspires an active, full, adventuresome life on the pathway to peace. This understanding, from the depth of my praying imagination, is: All I want is to be right here, right now, in this storm, with you.

Epilogue: Praying with Beads

I pick up the pace as I crest the ridge and head back down. I'm on the Three Tanks Trail in the Rincon Mountains, close to my home in Tucson, Arizona. The trailhead is less than four miles from my home. On long run days, this allows me to start in my neighborhood, run to the end of the road and then head up, into the mountains, on the single track, Douglas Springs Trail, which on this day, will lead me to Three Tanks. As I begin to run down, I look ahead and see an object in the trail that is too patterned to be a rock or twig. It rears its head and rattles its tail, a Western diamondback rattler, warning me not to get too close. Since I'm in no hurry, I stop and look… maintaining a respectful distance. I have a hearing loss, so the rattle is silent to me, which makes it even more interesting to watch it move. It's moments like this that call me to the deepest appreciation of the earth, movement, my body, and the Creator of all that is…we are one. This is a prayer. But I can't do this kind of prayer every day. Few can. There is work to do, grandchildren to care for. I am retired, Ann is not.

On the days when I cannot run in the mountains or go long miles on my bike, I sit cross-legged on the floor of my study and I pray. On days like this, I search for ways to integrate prayer and movement, spiritual energy, surprising observations, and the still center of my longing. For decades I have been intentional, as I develop the discipline required to seek the Holy in the profane. In short, I ask: how do I practice the discipline of prayer on those days I cannot go to the mountains? How do I practice in stillness?

Sitting on the floor of my office, rotating beads between my fingers, in the silence of my heart I speak, Jesus, let me be compassion and love. Then I become specific and pray Jesus, let me be compassion and love to. For twenty to thirty minutes, I prayerfully consider this desire to be made into something new by recognizing the active presence of the Spirit in my life.

It is not the same as running, but there is much here I can learn.

I grew up in South Jackson, Mississippi, a very protestant South Jackson, Mississippi. The only thing I knew about praying with beads was that Catholics prayed with rosaries. In my parochial world, Catholics were from Louisiana, spoke Creole in accents too thick to understand, ate crawfish, and drank beer. The only Catholic person I knew well was my grandfather who was from New Orleans and who had, in the pre-Vatican II era, been excommunicated for marrying my once-divorced Methodist grandmother. He kept a plastic statue of Mary on the dashboard of his truck. When I asked him about it, he matter of factly replied, "It's the Mother of God." I had no idea what that meant. In our deep Southern Methodist Church, we only mentioned Mary on Christmas Eve, and although I knew she was the mother of Jesus, she did not carry the significance afforded her by the title 'Mother of God'. In this environment, praying with beads had a magic feel to it, as if those who followed this practice believed the beads themselves carried some kind of unspoken power. We did not talk about things like that in church, or in the cab of his truck.

After all, we looked at Louisiana, where all the Catholics came from, with deep suspicion, somewhat like a foreign country. As you cross the border from south Mississippi to south Louisiana, the sides of the road are no longer gravel but become crushed shell, and Mardi Gras is a religious festival where people get drunk, then spend forty days saying they are sorry.

When I was small, my grandfather carried a rosary in his pocket. I never saw him do anything that looked like prayer with it. I only saw it when he pulled out his pocketknife and the rosary got in the way. I didn't know the magic words, and never heard him speak them.

Decades later, when I was on a retreat with the program staff from St. Paul's United Methodist Church and we were identifying our individual pathway to peace, I became frustrated with my inability to be still and pray. All of my life I had heard the Methodist admonition to daily devotions, private time with God. The cultural standard seemed to be thirty minutes a day; pick a time, same time every day. A few minutes reading the Bible, a bit of other spiritual reading and prayer. Uggggg prayer. Who could not like prayer? I didn't. It's not easy to admit how deep a struggle this was for me. There always seemed to be something I could not quite grasp. My relationship with the Holy was real enough, but prayer…it was like I was standing on the edge of a crowd, shouting, unnoticed. Throughout my life I have often felt compelled by the Spirit to think and do certain things: To find ways to care for the powerless, to welcome the stranger, to speak words of hope, and to believe these things were initiated by God. Careful attention to personal holiness and acts of piety all make sense to me. It's the act of praying that's a bit like walking along the tide line, knowing I am surrounded by beauty while constantly being knocked off balance.

Sit down in a quiet place…

What's that sound? Did I close the door?

Learn to meditate…

Is my time up yet?

Make prayer part of the daily devotion…

What will distract me today?

Pray the Rosary…

I looked up the words, and I have no idea what they mean.

Play spiritual, meditative music…

Does it count if I sing along? I can tap out the rhythms as I pray…is that okay? Look, a bird! Who is out there? My back is tired. My legs are going to sleep. Is it time to…?

One day, I went to Bookman's, our local used-book store, and perused the shelves for books about praying. Could there be any left I had not read? Yes! Praying with Beads, with the cover torn off along with the title page. Taped together and on sale for $1. I bought the tattered book and learned that Catholic and Orthodox Christians have a long practice praying with beads. Buddhists, Hindus, and Muslims do, too. Jewish believers count knots on the edges of prayer shawls. Though I was not sure what it was, surely all these many millions of people have something to teach me about prayer.

On our retreat, as others identified their personal pathway to peace, I identified the seven steps that sparked my praying imagination. We practiced various ways of praying through this, but mostly each of us identified steps, one by one, named them and tried to follow this cycle of prayer. I began to write a sermon series, "Praying the Pathway to Peace," that followed my seven steps, which are the organizational pattern for this book.

Still the question persisted, how did I best practice this myself if I weren't in motion? How did I pray if I wasn't moving? As an act of spiritual integrity, I needed to sort this out.

Jim Moffett is a friend and colleague who directs our ministry to the oldest members of our church and who also works with people in recovery from addiction. Jim is an artist and an educator. Jim is as movement oriented as I am, so he understands this lifetime struggle. One morning he came in my office and presented me with a gift, a string of beads circled into a bracelet. Jim suggested that it might become a helpful guide for me as I pray. I thanked him, and after he left I sat on the office couch and began to rotate the beads with my fingers as I moved from one to the other. As I did, I entered prayer. I touched each bead, and as I did so, I immediately felt myself relax and was surprised to find that this simple motion, fingering the beads as I moved through prayer, dissipated much of my nervous energy. I was able to focus as I prayed.

He had given me seven beads to represent the seven markers on my pathway to peace. Each day and countless times during worship on Sunday, I gently finger these beads, twisting them between my thumb and forefinger as I pray. Each bead has a story. As I pray, each story touches me, subconsciously informing the prayer. These stories insure that my spiritual practice is not just isolated and private, but that it connects with a larger world. This bridge links their history to the present moment of prayer and helps me identify the path to the still center. Praying with these beads not only calms my spirit, but they provide a link between me and my Roman Catholic, merchant-marine grandfather and his Italian family who lived much of their lives on the edge of New Orleans's French Quarter. Subtly, I become connected to the historical past, to international traders, great adventurers who wandered the world long before it was easy or common. My life and spirit are related to them all. The beads they used for trade are now wrapped around my wrist, warm and familiar, yet at the same time, foreign and provocative. I am connected with the peoples who have journeyed to new lands, trading, for hundreds of years all around the globe. Do the beads link me to my own nomadic spirit? Are my beads a way to focus not just on the prayer, but also to the literal history of wanderers? "Foxes have dens and birds have nests but the Son of Man has no place to lay his head." I have as much assurance as material wealth can offer, yet nurture a wandering spirit that sometimes causes me to feel rootless in the world. The creators of my beads offer a praying connection to both of those worlds.

And so I acknowledge… Prayer begins with silence.

The first bead is a blue-faceted Russian bead. These were made in China and traded by Russians into northwest North America. This bead is at least two hundred years old. These Russians beads were so sought after by the indigenous people of what became the northwestern United States that the beads brought for trade by Lewis and Clark were deemed inferior and ignored. I can imagine Russian sailors, over two hundred years ago, using these beads to forge introductions between themselves and the indigenous people of the Northwest Coast.

Could these beads create a connection between myself and the ancients? I sit alone and in silence, twisting the bead and repeating these words, "Prayer begins with silence." Sometimes I do this for long periods of time. Sometimes, especially in worship on Sundays, I do it rather quickly just to focus my thinking and to draw me back into the moment. When time permits, I do this until at last I can silence the restless voices in my head! Eventually, even the Russians leave, the folks whose disruption peppers my daily life, and even the room around me becomes quiet. The connection becomes my own silent prayer.

Silence leads to the love of God.

I move down the string of beads. The second bead, though bright red, is known as a white heart. White hearts come in many colors, yet they are all lined with an interior white coating that is visible from the outside. First made in the early 1400s in Venice, Italy, this bead is certainly over one hundred years old. White hearts have been historically valuable for trade in parts of Africa. I have been to Liberia twice and each time have looked, unsuccessfully, for these beads, yet I feel a river of affirmation for my African friends and the lessons they have given me as I rub this bead with my fingers, praying the words, Silence leads to the love of God. I try to open myself to the heart and to remember that silence allows the creativity that leads me to something new.

The love of God leads to the love of my neighbor.

The third bead is a chevron bead. These were first made in Venice in the early 1500s and are known as the 'Queen of Beads'. Mine is a red, white, and blue, elongated, modern reproduction, made in India. Chevrons as large as baseballs were hung by Arab traders from the corners of camel saddle blankets to help keep the blankets in place. I wonder about the nomadic nature of these traders, the chevrons carried over the trade routes, the literal paths of civilizations. Could their rotating motion, hanging from blankets thrown over camels, have lulled the traders into a peaceful means of prayerful travel? Or perhaps they became anchors for a journey of faith, holding something in place that would otherwise fall away? As the fantasy of travel fades from my mind, I find I can be specific in naming those people who are neighbors to me that require unusual intentionality for me to love them. They too are anchors for a journey that is rediscovered every day of parish life. The person who continually speaks of me in an unkind manner and leaves me challenged to find a faithful resolution is in the chevron's prayers. Jesus, chevron, who calls me to love my enemies, and then leaves me with the task of identifying them, so that I can become specific in my loving response.

The love of my neighbor leads to repentance.

As I finger this next bead, I am well aware of people who I do not know how to love. One thousand flowers, it is called. I pray that I can tell the truth about this struggle in one thousand ways. Once again, I name and think deeply into compassion for those who stretch my capacity to love. I wonder who finds it a struggle to love me. Is there ever a time in life when we can fully move beyond this emotional turmoil? If so, I have not arrived there.

Repentance leads to grace.

The bead is one of two differently colored Vaseline beads. These opaque beads were first made around 1914 and contain quantities of uranium salts. They became popular after Madame Curie discovered radium and people began to believe that wearing radium jewelry brought positive health benefits. They do glow under ultraviolet light! As I rub them, I long for the brightest light imaginable.

Repentance leads to grace is the light of the Christian faith. We are loved, forgiven, and allowed to grow in faith, not because we deserve it, earn it, achieve it, or learn it but because, as an act of grace, God has chosen to live in relationship with us.

Grace leads to generosity.

More light in the dark. The second bead. What I have learned is that though these beads fluoresce, the vitrification 'traps' the uranium inside the glass. The light splays out, but it does not contain enough uranium salt

236

to harm you. Thus, the meditation is ongoing, the light passing out through the glass without injury, only constantly giving off a metaphor for generosity. One who is aware of receiving this grace will always, as a first response, offer it freely to others, becoming fluorescent, so to speak.

Generosity leads to peace.

The final bead is yellowed and made from marine ivory, probably from the tusk of a walrus on the northwest coast of North America. Its age is unknown, and it was certainly made before our current consciousness about beleaguered marine species. It comes from the sea, the world of fluid mystery and beauty. It offers a source of confidence that the unseen world connects with my world in powerful and lasting ways. When I find myself touching this bead, I remember that mystery and beauty are all wrapped in the arms of grace. As I receive grace and offer it to others, I am led toward peace. I can never achieve an absolute level of peace. So even as my spirit relaxes, I find myself returning to the first, prayer begins with silence.

Seven beads, seven steps on the pathway to peace, seven markers along the way of the glaciated storms of my life, seven small beauties to direct my praying. During any given cycle of praying, one step may take minutes while another lasts just seconds. Most often when I get to the end, I am not through praying, but I am calm. As I continue to pray, I roll the beads in my fingers. The simple act of focused movement helps me concentrate. The coiled, rattling snake of my brain is not a source of fear, but is a source of disruption to be recognized and respected. The jawbone of a moose, lying beside the jawbone of a carnivore, cradles a mystery that can never be answered with assurance. Still, I don't want to disrupt it. In my mind, I let the light that has no words catch it and reflect. And the wildflowers sprouting between the few remaining teeth remind me that life and death are always in motion, always moving to an unseen horizon where hope waits. I run out of words.

Prayer begins with silence.